The Way I See It

Stories and Lessons Learned From 25 Years Behind the Turntables/Decks/Laptops

Michael J. Lenstra

THE WAY I SEE IT

ISBN 9781790353545

Proofreader: Chris Feldman

Printed in USA by KDP/Amazon Printing

For my wife and children

Past article comments:

"Just a short note to let you know I enjoy reading your column in Disc Jockey News."
– Jim Cerone, The Perfect Host

"Your article makes me want to print a billion copies and deliver them as an airborne leaflet."
- DJ Fly Robin Fly.

"Beautifully written my friend."
- Bill Hermann, Manager, The Entertainment Experience Workshop

"WOW! That was spot on."
- John Deggendorf, Pulse Productions

"[Your article] is so cerebral"
-Michael Buonaccorso, co-founder, Mobile Beat Magazine

"I love the analogy that you showed…"
-Glenn Mackay, G&M Event Group, Australia

Table of Contents

Introduction

Foreword

Section I A Different Way of Seeing Things

Chapter 1 Now It's a Party . . . Cheers! 1

Chapter 2 Just Say No! 5

Chapter 3 Play Nice With Everyone 11

Chapter 4 Lessons From the Donald 17

Chapter 5 What Does Smokey Know About DJing? 21

Chapter 6 Why I Didn't Play Your Request 23

Chapter 7 Things We Could Learn 29

Section II Views on the Industry

Chapter 8 Getting Better in the New Year 35

Chapter 9 Technical Difficulties 39

Chapter 10 Where Do We Find Today's Hits? 45

Chapter 11 Following Through 51

Chapter 12 Has the Needle Moved? 57

Section III Personal Experiences

Chapter 13 Misfortune Turns to Good Fortune 79

Chapter 14 It's the Secret Ingredient 83

Chapter 15 Expectations of the Mobile DJ Grow 89

Chapter 16 You Must Like Me 95

Chapter 17 It Pays to Be Nice 99

Chapter 18 Why Are You Here 103

Section IV Final Thoughts

Chapter 19 It's an Age-Old Question 109

Chapter 20 Sometimes a Mind Changes 115

Epilogue

Acknowledgments

Introduction

I met Mike Lenstra in the late 1990s through his wife, Laurie. She and I worked at the same prepress publishing house, and our work spaces were right next to each other. One day in passing I mentioned how when I was younger I had considered DJing for parties with a friend of mine, but the timing never worked out. She informed me her husband was a DJ, got me in touch with him, and the next thing I knew I was accompanying Mike on a pair of back-to-back events on a Saturday, the latter a dance at my old high school. I only remember two things about that day: (1) The movie *Armageddon* had recently come out, and for some reason "Leaving on a Jet Plane" by Chantal Kreviazuk from the movie's soundtrack went over really big with the high school crew, even though it really wasn't a big chart hit, and (2) I seemed to have a knack for mixing songs together that surprised Mike given that I was new at that. However, I didn't like talking on the microphone (still don't), and I marveled at how well Mike seemed to interact with the crowd, knowing just the right words to say and when in the songs to say them, like that long guitar solo in AC/DC's "You Shook Me All Night Long."

Since that time my role in Mike's company, Alexxus Entertainment, has evolved from DJ assistant to DJ subcontractor, to primarily working with Mike on his "Pop Quiz" game show.

Over the past few years as I've focused on my editorial career, I've mainly served as a resource person, someone to provide Mike with an occasional category for his Trivingo (trivia bingo) events, look up information, bounce ideas off of, and edit his monthly articles for the *Disc Jockey News*. Over the past 20 years or so, one thing has stood out to me about Mike: He's an excellent storyteller. Regardless of the situation, Mike has an entertaining way of talking about it. It's probably why he's such a natural as a DJ. I still remember learning how his company got its name (Alexxus, which was adapted from Alex [his son] and us [Mike and his wife]). My favorite story was about the first DJ gig Mike did and how people kept asking him for songs by "this Darth guy," who turned out to be Garth Brooks. That's the other thing . . . Mike knows his stuff, but he doesn't take himself too seriously. If he goofs something up, he'll admit it, usually with a laugh. It's just part of the story.

And it's been great watching him and his company evolve. He's really seen the DJ industry from all sides, from being a guy working part-time for somebody else's multi-op, to running his own DJ company, to seeing that grow into a multi-op, to eventually leaving his 9-to-5 job and making DJing his full-time career, along the way supplementing wedding receptions and school dances with game shows, trivia events, and marriage ceremonies. And now he has the opportunity to pass on the lessons he's learned through his *Disc Jockey News* articles. Granted, not everything he's tried has been a runaway success—the giant wheel originally used in his game show and the singles nights that never really expanded beyond a handful of people stand out—but he's never been afraid to try something new, and those ended up being nothing more than speed bumps in his career. Through it all he's also managed to maintain a happy and healthy marriage and family life . . . no small feat in itself.

Granted, I may be biased in my opinion, but the area has taken notice as well: For eight straight years, Alexxus Entertainment has won the Wedding Wire's Couples' Choice Award, and for the past five years Alexxus has been named the area's Best DJ in the annual Best Fest competition. And now he can add "author" to his resume. Given his varied life experience, I still hold out hope someday we'll see the Mike Lenstra autobiography, because there are many more stories to tell, but for now we have this collection of his favorite and most popular articles from his *Disc Jockey News* tenure to date. I hope you enjoy these as much as I have.

Chris Feldman

February, 2019

Foreword

I've always been fond of writing. I remember as a child writing stories and entertaining my mother and her girlfriends. That's not to say I wasn't a rambunctious child, far from it, but still I loved to put together a good tale. In junior high school I remember being given an assignment to write about the challenges the prisoners of war returning from Vietnam faced. I did it in a comical, first person piece. The social studies teacher was so impressed that, after I read it aloud, he wanted to share it with the other classes—which was a bit of a problem since, truth be told, I had not finished it. I just did an outline of the last two paragraphs and winged it for my oratory presentation.

In high school my interest was in creative writing and journalism, although after a couple of articles for the school newspaper I tired of that format (just the facts, please). After college it was a continuing education course with author John Tigges . . . and then I put the pen to rest for years. Work, marriage, and children left no time for writing. It would be nearly 20 years before one of the publications I subscribed to, *Mobile Beat* magazine, invited readers to send in stories of their most extraordinary events. I quickly did just that, and my story was published in the following issue. A few years later a local magazine was conducting a writing contest. I submitted a story and never heard from them—until they sent me a copy of the magazine with my published article and a check. Months later I found out I had placed second in that contest.

I've also always been a fan of pop music. My earliest recollection of listening to Top 40 hits was when I was 8 or 9 years old, listening to Al Sampson during the evening hours on 1490, WDBQ, on a dial tuned single speaker radio in Dubuque, Iowa. Back then the chart toppers were acts like Gary Puckett and the Union Gap, the Supremes, and the Association.

A few years later I made a point to listen to Casey Kasem and the American Top 40 every Sunday afternoon. I would record my favorite songs on a cassette and make my own, personal top 10 favorites list each week. In high school I had a classmate who got hired to spin tunes at a local bar on the weekends (drinking age was 18 back then, can you believe that?). "How do you get into that?" I asked. As a freshman in college I discovered that a fellow English student was the weekend DJ for the Ala Ka Zazz, our town's newest hot nightspot and first ever disco. "Why would he be going to college when he has the coolest job in town?" I thought.

I asked DJs at weddings I attended on how to get in the business. I actually applied at a company, but didn't hear anything in reply. Eventually, after a year of marriage when my wife and I were expecting child number one, we decided that with the upcoming expenses of diapers, bottles, day care, and who knew what else, maybe one of us should look into getting a part-time job to help supplement the family income. The next day I looked in the Help Wanted section of our local newspaper and there it was: Local company seeks DJs for private parties. Thus started my DJ career.

Twenty years later, by which point I owned my own Mobile DJ company, I picked up my latest edition of the *Disc Jockey News* and read Jeff Richards' column *Starting From Scratch*. One of his earlier columns was instrumental in inspiring me into making the jump to becoming a full-time performer. This article, though, was Jeff saying goodbye. He had moved on from the DJ world a few months earlier and had submitted his last column. And I thought, there must be an opening there for a writer, so armed with the confidence I had gotten from being published in my early endeavors I reached out to John Young, publisher of the *Disc Jockey News,* and inquired if he had any openings on his writing staff. I also sent John a couple of short stories that I had ideas for.

John wrote back. "I like those stories. Short, to the point, and things that make you go hmmm," he said. The next month one of those stories appeared as my first column.

What you're reading is a collection of those stories as they appeared in the *Disc Jockey News*—what I like to call my Greatest Hits album. More than just an accumulation of my seven years as a staff writer for the *Disc Jockey News,* it is a celebration of my 25 years as the owner of my own DJ business Each column is highlighted by a lesson that I have learned—and I hope that I've been able to pass some of these onto you and in some way made a difference—or at least made you think.

Driving home one night from a wedding, I was listening to talk radio on an AM station. Conservative radio host Joe Pags was leading a discussion, apparently right after one of the terrorist attacks in London. Joe had a daughter living in England and said he was asked by a friend if he feared for her safety.

"No," I remember Joe saying, because his daughter did not live in London but elsewhere in the country.

"What happens in London is really not reflective of life elsewhere in the country," he explained. "No more so than what happens in New York or L.A. is not reflective of America. If you want a microcosm of America you have to go to the suburbs."

He then decided to be more specific. "If you want a microcosm of America you have to go to Dubuque."

How ironic, I thought, as I was driving, that I was born, raised, and still live in Dubuque!

So, you may not entirely agree with my thoughts and opinions, but they come from someone living in Dubuque, the microcosm of the country . . . as Joe Pags sees it.

Right or wrong, agree or disagree, it's just the way I see it.

Michael J. Lenstra

SECTION I:

A Different Way of Seeing Things

Chapter 1

Now It's a Party . . . Cheers!

Author's Note: This article is very significant to me because it was the first one I had published once I started writing for the Disc Jockey News. *All these years later, I think the message . . . like the TV show it was based on . . . still holds up.*

(November 2011) I never have been much of a TV watcher. There are only a couple of shows I have ever made it a point to try and make time to sit down and watch. One of those was the very successful comedy *Cheers,* which is the basis for this month's article.

In this particular episode, titled "Friends, Romans, Accountants," one of the bar's regulars, Norm, was in charge of organizing his company party. The theme he chose was a toga party, and he got to work making plans. The night of the party, Norm bursts through the door of the bar and screams "Toga!" only to discover the bar is full, but dead silent, and no one is wearing a sheet. There have been livelier funerals. Even as the band that Norm hired strikes up the music, everyone groans.

"I don't understand it," Norm says. "They sounded so good on the phone."

To make a long story short, Norm's boss makes a play for the

Cheers cocktail waitress, Diane, and Norm has to intervene, which costs him his job. News of the altercation spreads through the bar like a flash fire.

"Norm, is it true you punched out the boss?" his co-employees ask. And suddenly it is a party! The energy level explodes, party revelers begin dancing, and the band now sounds fantastic!

And, as DJs, how many times have we been that band? How many times have we been a victim—or a benefactor—of circumstances that we had absolutely no control over at an event? There are times when a stressed bride is already tired of her wedding day before she ever sees us at the reception, or inter-office politics have put the employees in a no fun mood when they show up for that annual holiday party.

Truth is we're never as bad as we feel sometimes or as good as we think we are.

And how does the DJ come off looking in these situations?

On the other side of that coin, there are times when the wedding party is wound up and ready to go, or a school dance has a student body that will just dance to anything, and don't we look good then?

Truth is we're never as bad as we feel sometimes or as good as we think we are. We're somewhere in the middle, although I hope we're closer to the latter.

The way I see it, as professional DJs it is as much our responsibility to recognize these situations and be able to defuse the bad ones and play off the good ones as it is to carry thousands of songs, state of the art equipment, and pack the dance floor. It's these situations that separate the true professional DJs from those that "just push play."

Chapter 2

Just Say No!

(August 2016) Meghan Trainor sings about it. Nancy Reagan built an anti-drug campaign around it. It may be one of the earliest words we learn as children. Even so, it is one we hesitate to use when dealing with customers, even though it can be very beneficial at times.

The word is *no.*

There was a time when I used *no* far, far less than words like *OK* or *absolutely* when it came to dealing with clients, but time has changed my view. The following story should help explain why.

A little earlier this year I was finishing up a wedding and packing the gear in my truck when my phone rang. It was another local DJ.

"Mike, where was your wedding at tonight?"

I told him where I was and he was relieved, then went on to tell me about another wedding in town and the stories that were coming out about it. The word was there was a huge brawl. A pair of police officers were dispatched. They had to call for backup. By the time it was finally under control there were allegedly eight patrol cars there.

"Do you know who was there?" he asked.

"No," I replied, "but I know who the couple was . . . ."

About seven or eight months earlier I had gotten an e-mail from a couple inquiring about my services. "Yes, I'm available," I told them. "Would you like to get together and talk about your wedding day?"

We set a date to meet at their reception facility a few days later. It was the bride and groom, their two children, the bride's mother, and myself. I assumed the bride's mother came along to keep an eye on the little ones, though I wondered why she just did not stay at home with them, but I soon found out that mom would be calling the shots at this wedding. She inserted herself into the conversation, asked some questions, and then began to tell me horror stories from her other daughter's wedding from just a few months earlier.

It is probably more of our responsibility to convey what we can offer to our clients than it is to promise them everything just to get a booking.

Red flag number one.

Apparently, as mommy dearest tells it, daughter number one's wedding ceremony took place in a gazebo at a local park. As everyone gathered for the nuptials, one of the family members pulled out a smartphone to plug into the gazebo's sound system . . .

except there was none! "They [the local park division] never told us that!" the furious mother said. The ceremony proceeded with no music and from there they went to the reception where there WAS a sound system for their devices. However, halfway through the night no one was dancing, so the mother stepped up to the plate and located the room captain to let her know what corrective steps she needed to make to get the party started. For those reasons, they were not going back to that place for daughter number two's wedding.

Red flag number two.

As we got ready to wrap up our meet-and-greet, the mother asked me what the retainer fee would be, then stated, "I get paid the week after next, can you hold onto the date until then and I can write you a check?" Now, I'm not sure how you view this, but my thoughts are if you have to wait for several days for payday just to afford the deposit, this has all the warning signs of a wedding that is going to cancel, or someone who is going to try to renegotiate the price down the line, or someone who is not going to pay you at all. Another red flag. At that point, I started debating whether the event would be more trouble than reward. I didn't agree to anything immediately. Instead, I simply asked the couple to look over the information that I had given them and call me if they had any questions.

Nearly two weeks later they e-mailed me asking if I had sent a contract. I had to tell them that I discovered that their wedding was on the same day that I would be moving my daughter back from school. Although I probably could have adjusted some things to do the event, I decided in that case to help my daughter move instead and wished them well.

Yep, I said no.

I learned later from an employee at their reception venue that the groom's parents were divorced and it seemed that there were still some hostile feelings between the father and his ex-in-laws. Add a little alcohol into that and you have a recipe for a wedding that will be memorable—but for all the wrong reasons. I definitely made the right call.

I did not always have the fortitude to say no, but it has been a lesson that was learned with experience and some missteps. Not long after I founded my own company I booked a wedding for the daughter of the principal at my son's school, and it had all the signs of a good time. That is, until we all got together just weeks before the big day and the groom pulled out a small CD wallet. Seems he had been busy. In what probably took more time than I can imagine, he had burned a set of CDs (ah yes, the CD age) containing all of the songs he wanted to hear at his wedding—in the order he wanted them in! I tried to reason with him on two fronts. First, there would be a gap between each song since I would not have the ability to cross fade them on two different players.

And a bigger concern, what if no one was dancing? Oh, he assured me, they will dance.

And he was right—for about 30 minutes. He had some traditional favorites included in those early tracks, then he went down a weird road, including some obscure songs that only his college buddies and he had a connection to. Soon no one was dancing. "Do something!" he begged. "Do you want me to segue from the list?" I asked. "Well, no," was his response. I ended up using many of his songs, but not in the order that he had put them in. People danced, but I do not think he left his wedding reception a happy guy. Hopefully over the years he has thought of that and would approach the same scenario differently. I know I do.

Even with that knowledge, I continued to promise the world, but I did try to at least counsel people when they were going in a direction I did not think was in their best interest. A bride once met with me and told me that she wanted nothing but country music at her wedding.

"We can do that," I said, but then added, "but can you speak for all of your cousins and neighbors and coworkers and be assured that all they wish to hear is country music?" She softened a little and agreed to throw in some oldies, but then called me just days before her wedding and went back to her original plan. The reception was from 3:00 to 9:00, but by 7:40 they were taking all of the gifts out to the car, because everyone was gone. I guess there were not as many country music fans at her wedding as she thought. Lesson learned.

So it was without hesitation that I answered an e-mail recently in which a groom wrote and told me he just needed a DJ to introduce the wedding party, do some light emceeing, and play the music off of their list. "That is not what we do," I explained to him in the reply. I went on to tell him we need the flexibility to work in requests and go with what is motivating the crowd.

"Forget it," he wrote back. "If you think you know our guests better than we do . . . ."

But the truth is, we do. The way I see it, it is probably more of our responsibility to convey what we can offer to our clients than it is to promise them everything just to get a booking on our calendar.

Chapter 3

Play Nice With Everyone

(March 2015) The Academy Award-winning picture *Ordinary People* deals with a seemingly perfect American family and how they crumble in the wake of tragedy. In the climactic scenes of the movie, harsh words are exchanged:

"Can't you see anything except in terms of how it affects you!?" the husband screams. "No, I can't–and neither can you or anybody else!" retorts an angry wife.

Through that exchange, they may have stumbled onto the root of their problems.

But this column is not meant to be about movies or marriage advice, but rather about how we as Mobile DJs could help our cause a bit by seeing things in terms of not only how they affect us, but rather as a whole, particularly at weddings.

A fellow DJ and good friend of mine, and I'll call him Bob, because that's his name, and I talk all the time, sometimes right after our events on a Saturday night and maybe even a few times during the week. Most of our conversations center around shop talk, and in one of those conversations he mentioned giving advice to his nephew who was getting married.

"Wow, you should be a wedding planner with all that you know about weddings," his nephew said.

Or should he? Maybe Bob was giving advice on just how he see things in terms of how it affects us as Mobile DJs.

For years I would get frustrated with some of the other wedding vendors in our area: photographers who would want to rush through wedding traditions or take the bride and groom outside right after dinner just so they could get their pictures and be on their merry way–or banquet managers who couldn't care less what itinerary you had worked out with the bride and groom because they had their own. Once I started communicating with those professionals, though, I began to see things from their point of view. With that knowledge I began to ask other wedding professionals what frustrations they have working with co-wedding vendors on an event.

"A couple different photographers have gotten WAY too close and up in my (or my bandmate's) grill, stepping over cables and leaning over mic stands to get shots, making everyone nervous that they were about to knock something over," said Lindsay S., a vocalist and guitar player from Boston. "Another time a videographer asked me to move so she could have the spot I was in to shoot from! She then started picking up my equipment to help me move it even after I had asked her not to multiple times."

Sacramento florist Monique W. says dealing with time constraints has been a frustration: "The venue . . . books weddings back to back, and the florist is waiting to set the reception area while prior wedding die hard guests are still dancing or sitting at the tables, and the venue staff are too timid to throw them out. The florist then only gets maybe a half hour to set up."

New Jersey celebrant Celia M. has had several frustrations.

"Photographers who are dressed like slobs and then proceed to stand RIGHT NEXT to me or in front of the bridal party, obscuring the view of the groom/bride and the family. And they're in the video that way," she says, or "DJs who miss the recessional cue. It sounds small but it's really awkward to have that pause; any pro who is late, especially make-up artists who can delay the ENTIRE day. Shuttles/limos who get lost/arrive late/forget passengers; planners/day of coordinators who don't bother to contact me for any given detail about the ceremony; venue coordinators who don't coordinate, arrange the bridal party, or shepherd the process."

Another officiant, Nancy T. of Sarasota, Florida, has only one complaint: "I'm a female officiant who really doesn't need the male DJ mic'ing me—keep your hands to yourself!"

As for some of my issues with photographers, David D. of Wisconsin puts it this way: "In partial defense of the photographer that runs off with the wedding party and delays the meal, there have been times when the bride has asked for pictures that may have delayed things somewhat, but when the bride asks for something we go do it as quickly as possible." He continues,

"There are some DJs that seem to think that just because they are just getting started that we are as well, they don't understand that we may have been running around with the wedding party for the last six hours."

And his take on some of those in our profession?

"I have had lots of problems with DJs not giving me a heads up about toasts, first dance and that sort of thing, even after talking to them about their plans and asking them to do so. I've had a few that I told them I had to go out of the room for pictures or whatever and come back only to find the best man giving his toast or the couple doing their first dance already," he says. "Thankfully these guys are the exception and not the rule."

As for my dilemmas with the banquet staff, I learned early on that a call to them a few days before a wedding would get all of us following the same schedule.

We are all on a quest for the same goal.

In Madison, Wisconsin, the local chapter of the National Association of Wedding Professionals kicks off every year with a round table discussion featuring upcoming couples and just married newlyweds. "We set the room up to look like a wedding and we set the couples up at the head table," explains Ally Krezinski, current president of the chapter. Attendees are invited to write down questions, which are presented to the couples through an emcee. The questions are centered on what they are looking for in certain services as they are planning their wedding and what some of the deciding factors were in choosing the providers they did. "We try to keep [the names] anonymous as far as who they did decide to go with," explains Ally, thus keeping the event from being a promotional opportunity.

What a great concept! Not only does it provide those attendees with great feedback on where to advertise and what message your target client is looking for, but it also helps you see things through the eyes of your co-vendors, not to mention the networking opportunity.

The way I see it, we are all on a quest for the same goal–to provide our couples with a wonderful, memorable experience. By "playing nice with everyone," working together and seeing things from another person's vantage point, we can help ensure that.

If that couple from *Ordinary People* would have done so, maybe they could have lived happily ever after.

Chapter 4

Lessons From the Donald

Author's Note: I wrote this column in the early days of 2012
when the thought of Donald Trump as
president was considered comical. Who knew?

(April 2012) If you've read my first few articles, you've probably caught a recurring theme: *life is one big lesson.* If we just pay attention, there are many learning opportunities around us every day that we can utilize to improve both our business and our personal life. Yes, there are books, classes, and seminars that will take us there. But everyday situations may be just as effective a learning tool. So with that in mind, I am going back to TV land to none other than Donald Trump for this month's lesson.

In one of my first columns I stated that I do not watch much TV, but then I went on to describe what I learned from a classic well-known sitcom. I still maintain that the tube is not a big part of my daily life, but one show I do seem to take time out to watch is *The Apprentice.* For those of you who may not be familiar with it, let me give you the 10 cent synopsis: Each season nearly two dozen people are brought to Donald Trump's headquarters in hopes of becoming one of his well-paid apprentices. The individuals are grouped into two teams, and each week, both teams

17

are given the same task—most often to raise money. The team that wins is rewarded, and the losing team must face 'The Donald' and his advisors in his boardroom, where one of them will be "fired."

Just because you're busy does not mean you're making money.

It's season 5, and teams Gold Rush and Synergy are down to their final three contestants— the former is an all-male group while the latter is composed of females. Their task this week is to organize a tailgate party to be held at a Rutgers University football game. The team that can raise the most money will be declared the winner. The men of Gold Rush are off, securing exclusive rights of the Rutgers cheerleaders for their event and blanketing the campus with promotional flyers. The gals are consistently a step behind. Come the day of the event, the boys have it going on with their party, featuring an eating contest and an inflatable money machine, among other activities. The crowd is big and enthusiastic. The girls, meanwhile, are left to renting makeshift cheerleader outfits and providing car hop service in the parking lot with their food entrées.

Cut to judgment day in the boardroom. The gals of the Synergy team nervously file in, followed by a very smug Gold Rush squad. After reviewing both teams' approach the figures are revealed, and the winners are . . . the *ladies* of Synergy!

"How could this be so?" the shocked and dismayed guys ask. They clearly had the more popular event and the biggest crowd! But it all came down to simple math. You see, while the boys were partying it up with the college students, they were also selling their main entrées for $2, while the ladies' price point was more than double that for their food choices ($5), and there were enough people in the parking lot willing to pay the additional cost for the extra (car hop) service. The ladies are treated to a nice trip to a local winery, while the men are sent back into the boardroom to face the wrath of Donald Trump.

Think of how that relates to our business. How many times have we seen people in our local area or on social media state how busy they are? "Yep," they say. "I've got four events this week!" Then you find out they did a karaoke show on Thursday ($200), a junior high dance on Friday ($250), a wedding in the basement of the local union hall Saturday night ($500), and a gig for their niece's birthday party on a Sunday afternoon (well, that's a freebie, a chance to wow the relatives with his, or her, persona). Total take: $950.

Meanwhile, you've done a wedding Saturday ($995), where the couple also asked you to provide a sound system for the ceremony ($225), and then they decided to add some uplighting or gobo lighting ($200), all of which adds up to . . . well, you get the picture.

The way I see it—and I'm sure you do too—is that just because you're busy does not mean you're making money. Just ask the guys from Gold Rush.

Chapter 5

What Does Smokey Know About DJing?

(January 2012) Who is Henry "Smokey" Yunick? This racing legend, who died in May of 2001, was closely associated with motorsports, serving as a mechanic and car designer. He is probably best known for his time with NASCAR, where he worked as a mechanic, builder, and crew chief. In his later years, Yunick became a columnist for the racing publication *Circle Track* magazine, and I was one of his biggest fans.

In my life BMC (i.e., before marriage and children), racing was one of my main interests. As a subscriber of *Circle Track,* I would read Smokey's columns every month. All were insightful, but there was one column that has stuck with me for years. A reader had asked for advice on how to get his race car to go faster. Smokey gave him his usual answer: "The cost of speed is money." he wrote. "How fast you want to go depends on how much money you're willing to spend."

His final words, though, were the ones that made a lasting impression. He stated, "It depends on where you want to finish. If you're content on finishing in the back of the pack, get your advice from those who finish there. If you want to finish in the middle, then middle of the pack racers are the people you want to be talking to. But if you want to finish at the front, then those that consistently finish there are the people you should be getting your advice from."

What great advice—and it doesn't just apply to racing. Many Mobile DJs are not just entertainers or music masters, but also small businessmen. Fortunately, there has never been a time when so much information is available to help those of us in the profession grow and improve our businesses. In addition to industry-specific conventions, magazines, seminars, newspapers, and associations, we also have Facebook groups, marketing newsletters, e-books, and blogs.

"If you want to finish at the front, then those that consistently finish there are the people you should be getting your advice from."—Henry "Smokey" Yunick

The way I see it, we could all benefit by seeking out the leaders in our industry and taking advantage of the information that is so readily available to us, not only to improve ourselves and be front runners in our own communities, but also to continue to give our industry credibility. "Smokey" Yunick's words and example can help steer us to the front of the pack.

Chapter 6

Why I Didn't Play Your Request

(September 2018)

Dear Guest,

Word has reached me that you were upset because your request(s) were not played at a wedding where I recently performed. I do apologize that I was unable to play your song requests, and I feel compelled to give you some possible reasons why that may have happened.

First and foremost, I believe there is a misconception of what a professional DJ's role is at a wedding reception. Most believe we are there to play music, to be sort of a human jukebox and play the songs we are asked to, period. But in actuality our responsibilities are much broader than that. You see, we are most often hired to help create and lead a celebration. Typically, that requires fulfilling two different tasks. The first is to be the spokesperson for the couple, so to speak, and help guide their guests through the itinerary of the night, introduce the members of their wedding party, and give a personal introduction to anyone who will be using the microphone. Our second task is to finish the couple's wedding day off with a great celebration. To do this, yes, we play music, but much like a comedian uses jokes, or a magician uses illusion tricks, music is just the tool that we use to entertain. And like those two entertainment fields, the timing and how we use that tool is critical. For instance:

- If you were the guest who was asking for the latest tracks from Drake and Kendrick Lamar, but dinner was just concluding, my answer to you was "Yes" and "No." Yes, I do have those tracks, but no, right after dinner is not the ideal time to play them. Those types of artists generally appeal to younger guests and tend to go over better much later in the evening, after the party has been underway for a while.

- If you were the guest who asked, just after I had wrapped up a slow set and picked up the pace, that I go back and play another slow song next because you wanted to bring Grandma out to dance, again my answers were "Yes" and "No." Yes, I can do that, but no, I won't, because there is a timing issue. Most often music is programmed (they actually do the same thing in radio) and I have for years followed the 8/10–2 rule, which means I typically play 8 to 10 up-tempo songs before slowing it down for two slower songs. I almost never do less than two slow songs—that gives everyone a chance to find their dance partner and make their way to the floor, but I also almost never do more than two in a row because, again, it is a celebration and I want to get everyone back on the floor to party. Be patient, because another slow set is coming up and I will be sure to play something for Grandma.

- Perhaps you were the guest who asked me to play "Should've Been a Cowboy" for Uncle Charlie. I remember the story you told me of how a few of you went on a fishing trip and Uncle Charlie, after a few beers, started singing that song loud enough for most of the people in the campground to hear. This will be a hoot, I remember you telling me. That may be so, but this is not the place to have a "Gotcha" moment at Uncle Charlie's expense. This is the bride and groom's wedding day, and to put it on pause just so three or four of you can point at Uncle Charlie and enjoy an inside joke, well, this isn't the place. However, if you'd like to hire me to entertain at a party for Uncle Charlie where everyone can relive their favorite memories, I'm happy to give you my card and we can talk.

- Could it be that you were the guest who wanted the microphone to sing "Ice Ice Baby," and were upset that I would not give it to you even after you watched both the maid of honor and the stepbrother of the bride lead the charge on the mic when we played "Shoop" and "Baby Got Back," respectively? There was a reason that happened. You see, during my pre-planning meetings with the couple they asked me to play those songs and have those two sing along. The "Shoop"/maid of honor thing goes back to the bride and her maid of honor's college days, and the "Baby Got Back"/stepbrother scenario is one that the couple told me had gotten to be a tradition at all the family weddings. Those connections helped create a memorable moment for this couple, but it does not mean I'm allowed to turn their wedding reception into an open mic night.

• Now I'm wondering . . . were you one of those who asked me to play something from Red Wanting Blue or Poi Dogs Pondering? I'm actually familiar with both of those bands, but they are more popular in their local markets only, and most people will not dance to music they are not familiar with. This is a subject I bring up with every couple I meet with. "With your permission," I always ask, "Is it okay if I screen the requests out for two criteria? One, that it is within the genres that you have selected, and two, that it is DANCEABLE, because some people do not realize that what they like to listen to and what a lot of people will dance to are not always the same thing?" When I make that request, 100% of our couples have said YES. Mid-tempo and obscure songs tend to clear off the dance floor. There was a saying in the movie *Star Trek II: The Wrath of Khan* that went, "The needs of the many outweigh the needs of the few . . . or the one." If I play a song you really love, but I lose the rest of the dance floor in the process, I haven't fulfilled my duties of what the wedding couple expects of me. I have to consider everyone, not just what a few will enjoy.

• I do apologize if you were one of the half dozen guests who came to me in the last 40 to 45 minutes of the wedding and asked if I would play your slow song, with some of you telling me it was your wedding song. I wish I could play every such request. However, the average number of songs played per hour at an event is 15 to 16, which means in the last 40 minutes or so I only have time for a dozen—and I've already kept a few from the bride/groom's list until the closing minutes purposefully so we can finish with a bang. It's like the encore of a concert. The perfect scenario is to end the couple's wedding day with one last big hurrah—and playing a half dozen slow songs in the last 40 minutes of their celebration will not help me achieve that goal.

- Finally, if you were one of the guests who came over to me hurriedly and stated, "The bride just sent me over and asked me to have you play [insert song] NEXT!!" I could tell by the look on your face that that was not actually the case. I hear this line wedding after wedding after wedding, so now during my consultations with each couple I work out a password with them

First and foremost, I believe there is a misconception of what a professional DJ's role is at a wedding reception.

and if they indeed do send someone over they give that person the secret code. I did not do yours "next" because, let's be honest, I could tell by your blank look and surprise in your eyes when I asked for the password that the bride and groom never sent you over. This is not to say that I did not play any requests made of me during the event. Looking back at my sheet I see that I did play over a dozen. Those Shania songs, "Bust a Move," "Yeah" from Usher . . . yep, those were all requests, as were many others. A good number of the other selections I played came right from the couple's list that we compiled at their consultation.

It comes down to this: As DJs, we are judged by how successful the entire party is, and a good sign of that is how full the dance floor remains during the event. Yes, we do play music, but the way I see it, what we play and when we play it is critical in making the event a complete success. We will take requests, but they need to fit the overall program we have laid out, in the same way potato chips may go great at a cookout but not at a lobster dinner. I hope my letter gives you a better understanding of why one of your requests was not played. It certainly wasn't anything personal, dear guest.

And I hope my replies give you, the reader, something to think about as well.

Chapter 7

Things We Could Learn From the Oldest Profession

(February 2013) In their highly successful book series *Freakonomics,* authors Steven D. Levitt and Stephen J. Dubner give us a peek at, as their book's subtitle explains, the hidden side of everything, whether it is what caused the crime rate to drop in the 1990s, why drug dealers live with their mamas, or things you always thought you knew but didn't. Each conclusion is supported with data. "We give people permission to challenge conventional wisdom and ask a different kind of question entirely," says Dubner.

In their second book, *SuperFreakonomics,* Dubner and Levitt study the prostitution trade in Chicago and introduce us to Allie, a successful and highly paid "escort" on that city's western suburbs. It was noted in their study that Allie charged a fee that climbed to exceed nearly 10 times higher than that of the corner prostitute in the city's poorer neighborhoods.

But there's a reason.

The corner gals in the study were predominantly drug addicts who lived in the lower social economic status. Because of that, they seemed content with almost any reasonable fee that they could negotiate. In contrast, Allie had gone to college and spent time in the military. In addition, she was an attractive and well-kept lady. The workplace for the street corner ladies of the night was usually a seedy motel or a mattress in the basement of an apartment complex. By comparison, Allie maintained a nice, orderly, and finely decorated apartment where she entertained her clients. The men who visited the street corner prostitutes were mostly men of the same lower social economic status. The corner ladies were easy to spot because they usually wore track suits for, let's just say, ease of the job requirements. Allie's clients, however, were predominantly white collar professionals: bankers, lawyers, and real estate agents, and she dressed nice for them.

"Allie is essentially a trophy wife who is rented by the hour"
—Steven D. Levitt and Stephen J. Dubner

Essentially, all these women were offering sex for money. Moral questions aside, why, then, would a guy go to Allie and spend so much more when the same service was available for much less?

"For an hour or two, she [Allie] represents the ideal wife," the authors write. "Beautiful, attentive, smart, laughing at your jokes

30

and satisfying your lust. She is happy to see you every time you show up at her door. Your favorite music is already playing and your favorite beverage is on ice. She will never ask you to take out the trash.

"Allie is essentially a trophy wife who is rented by the hour," they surmise. "She isn't really selling sex, or at least not sex alone. She sells men the opportunity to trade in their existing wives for a younger, more sexually adventurous version–without the long term expense."

In essence, Allie is giving them the total experience of a fairytale relationship without the strings attached, which involves (but does not *entirely* involve) a sexual element. Because of this, the higher cost is totally acceptable to her customers.

By now you're probably asking, how does this relate to the DJ industry? We certainly don't offer the same services, not to mention perform what could be viewed as morally questionable ones. So what lesson can we learn from Allie? Simply put: Quality creates value, and value increases price. The concept is really not much different than selling a home or car. When selling a house, the first things sellers typically do is spruce it up, paying attention to the details. When selling a car, they shine it up and give it a tune-up, making it more attractive to potential buyers so they'll pay a higher price.

In Allie's business, her clientele were not just looking for sex. The woman on the street corner could provide that. They were looking for that, plus something more. And that "something more" justifies the higher price Allie charged. In our business, many of our customers are also focusing on quality and value. They don't just want some guy to play music. Anybody with a portable music device and a pair of speakers can do that. They too want the "total experience," the interaction with the crowd, the knowledge of what gets people dancing, the extra attention. So time spent worrying about the craigslist DJ may be time wasted, when we instead could be focusing it on refining the quality of our service and increasing our value to attract the customer that values it.

"Allie had mastered her domain," conclude the authors. "She was a shrewd entrepreneur who kept her overhead low, maintained quality control, learned to price discriminate and understood well the market forces of supply and demand."

Am I suggesting that you search out a prostitute or take up the occupation in the name of job research? No, but in terms of careers, ours is a relative newbie and, the way I see it, we could still learn a few pointers from the world's oldest profession. The added value comes in the details and the "something more."

What "something more" can you give your clients through your customer service and your product to increase your bottom line and become as successful in business as Allie?

SECTION II:

Views on the Industry

Chapter 8

Getting Better in the New Year

(January 2015) A funny thing has happened to me in the last couple of years (not funny ha ha but funny peculiar, just to be clear). Every time I've raised my price I've gotten busier. First it was another $50 on each event, then it went to an extra $100. Last year I decided to up my company's standard event price by $200 per wedding. "I don't know about that," said one of my associates. "That might be a bit of a jump." But my logic was simple: A survey I read revealed that an estimated 30% of engaged couples had avoided getting married in the year 2013 because of the "bad luck factor" associated with the number 13. I was certain—and research backed up my hunch—that 2014 was going to be a busy year in the wedding industry. Since that's where the majority of my business comes from, it seemed to be an opportune time to raise my rates to coincide with the expected increase in demand. My theory proved correct. Despite the price increase, it was my company's second busiest wedding season ever. (The record was set in 2012, which I also attributed to many couples trying to get their wedding in before 2013, the "year of the snake.")

You might think, is image in the eye of the beholder? In other words, because I'm paying more I'm getting more? Some of that might be true. Several years ago I read a story where a brand of vacuum cleaner had entered into the market and did very well. After they had exceeded their business plan's expectations, they decided to be a bit more competitive and lower their prices—and when they did sales dropped. They raised the cost back up to their original price point and, to their surprise, sales returned to normal. I shared this story with a coworker who was just about to have a garage sale that coming weekend. The following Monday he told me as he was ready to wrap up his event he surveyed what was left and noted a coffee maker had not sold. His first inclination was to mark the price down before the end of his sale, but then he remembered the story I had told him, so instead he raised the price . . . and it sold within minutes.

Now, the moral of this story may seem simple: raise your prices and your business will actually grow, not decline. While that may be somewhat true, there is a second part to the equation I should explain. You see, every time I've given myself a raise I felt I needed to justify that somehow, maybe by updating equipment, my website, or my bridal show set-up. However, most of this improvement has been done by searching for ways that I can be a better DJ. I worked on making my presentation to clients stand out more and began to offer more unique and creative ideas to not only meet, but exceed their expectations. I've spent hours reading business-related magazines and blogs and scanning the many DJ-related Facebook groups. On my bookshelf you will find DVDs and audio CDs from heavyweights in our industry like Randy Bartlett, Peter Merry, Ron Ruth, Mitch Taylor, Dan Nichols, and Scott Faver. My inbox is filled with marketing e-mails from wedding experts Rick Brewer, Alan Berg, Chris Jaeger, Stephanie and Jeff Padovani, and sales guru Jeffrey Gitomer, just to name a few. I cannot tell you the name of another band member from Maroon 5 other than Adam Levine and no one from One Direction or even what the name of any of their albums are, but I can tell you who authored *The Best Wedding Reception Ever* and who the creator of the *1% Solution* is. In short, I've spent way more of my efforts on marketing and professional development than I have on music knowledge or what the specs of my equipment are—and the results seem to be paying off.

Every time I've given myself a raise I felt I needed to justify that somehow.

What about you? What have you been doing to up your game? What are your goals for the new year? Rick Brewer of GetMoreBrides.com is fond of saying "a better lifestyle is sometimes only $5,000 away, which may be only five or six more events a year." How can you add those events to your calendar? I believe the answer is—at least in part—education, and as our industry evolves more and more into a recognizable industry with so many more people choosing to be a Mobile DJ as their primary source of income, more educational opportunities have arisen. There are the DJ conventions like Mobile Beat Las Vegas, Midwest DJs Live, and the ARMS DJs. There's also the annual DJ Expo, typically held in Atlantic City each August.

Added to those are specific industry-related seminars like the Lighting Symposium that is organized by NLFX owner Ben Stowe and held in Minneapolis in early spring, or the Wedding MBA, held in Las Vegas in the fall.

Many of these educational opportunities are preceded or followed with workshops that are put on by the aforementioned industry experts, like Peter Merry's "Make It Grand" or "The Professional Process," or Randy Bartlett's "Advanced Microphone Techniques." There is also Mark Ferrell's MC or Love Story Workshops and Bill Hermann's "Entertainment Experience" for those seeking to keep improving.

The way I see it, with so many avenues to keep learning and improving available to the Mobile DJ today it only takes a bit of drive on our part to seek those out and take our performance to the next level. Who knows, if you suddenly find yourself overwhelmed by success you can always *lower* your price.

Chapter 9

Technical Difficulties

(April 2014)

THE GOOD EVIL

Technology: Is it a cure-all or a curse? In many cases, it's different sides of the same coin. As members of the Mobile DJ community, we have benefited from several industry-related inventions over the past 20 years, such as digital music, LED lighting, and the super information highway known as the Internet. But what have other technological advances cost us? In a recent article titled "Death of the High School Dance," *New York Post* contributor Caroline Moss observed that her high school, which held several dances a year attracting up to 800 students while she was there in 2001, now only holds one, the Prom, because of a lack of interest and attendance (the Homecoming dance in 2010 only drew 26 students). What could cause such a drastic change in only nine years?

"Kids don't need to go to a dance to interact with each other when they can sit in their bed with their laptop and phone and text them," explained Moss's younger sister, a current student at the same school. "You don't have to show up to a dance hoping to see someone anymore. You can literally Snapchat them and see them on Snapchat. It's basically like being with that person."

Ah yes, social media, the everything answer for personal interaction in the 21st century.

BLAME IT ON EDISON

Technology has taken the blame for a lot in the past 60 years. The invention of the television was accused of taking up a lot of America's family time. Video games were vilified for shifting kids' outside playtime, transferring them instead to the front of a TV screen. Today smartphones and computers are listed as the culprit for many of us being socially inactive and/or physically unfit—or for the disappearance of the school dance.

"Just because technology allows for us to do something doesn't mean it's the right thing to do."—Brian Beez

WHAT'S ON THE HORIZON?

A new form of technology is creeping into the Mobile DJ world. Services or apps like *FireText* or *DJ Song Request* are giving guests the ability to text the DJ their request rather than walking up to the person and verbally communicating that. One of those services, *RequestNow,* puts it this way: "Eliminate the need for slips of paper, unintelligible handwriting, and conversations over blasting speakers that distract you from your set." Alleviating the need to deal with less than sober guests is another benefit noted. At the risk of painting myself as an old person unable to accept change, I see several problems with these services:

- A tool like this can be abused by the socially inactive guest who has no intention of being on the dance floor, but passes his or her time requesting several songs to the DJ.

- Youths may decide to flood the system with their favorite songs. In the early days of my DJ career, the company I worked for had thousands of request tents printed up and we were required to place them on every table at our events. The problem it caused was that many of the 'tweeners in attendance would kidnap them all and fill them out nearly exclusively with songs from their favorite boy bands of the day, in essence "stuffing the ballot box" and not giving a true representation of what everyone there really wanted to hear.

- We lose the ability to interact with guests. Relationship building is still a major part of our business.

- We are unable to discuss things with clients. How many times have you had a guest approach you and ask for a song that you just knew was not going to be a floor packer ("Creeping" by Eric Church is one that comes to my mind)? However, in talking to the guest, maybe you could persuade him or her that a song like "Drink in My Hand" by that same artist may be a better choice.

• Guests may expect to hear their request right away. Had they walked up to you and requested it, you might have had the chance to explain to them that this particular client gave you an extensive list of songs that they wanted to hear and so those were a priority—or maybe their request was on the client's DO NOT PLAY list.

One of my associates, Brian Beez, looks at it this way: "My first reaction is that [texting requests] sounds very impersonal. Plus you don't know who the request came from, so if you don't play it or don't have it you can't talk with them—explain—and ask them if they have another request. While the incidences of dealing with difficult people do occur, they pale in comparison to the total number of people that you interact with positively at an event. In the grand scheme of things, I'll take the few jerks for the dozens and dozens of folks that simply want to interact with you and see if you'll play their song. Plus, I just think the texting thing adds an added task to attend to." He continues, "Just because technology allows for us to do something doesn't mean it's the right thing to do. Others may disagree but I pride myself on being as friendly and personable as possible while I perform, and I believe that goes a lot farther in making for happy customers than the convenience of texting."

Well-known Mobile DJ Randy Bartlett explained in one of his seminars why he never carries signage or broadcasts his company name at a wedding. "I'm perfectly confident in their (the guests) ability to get up, walk over, and ask for a card," he says.

The way I see it, I feel just the same way in their ability to request a song.

Chapter 10

Where Do We Find Today's Hits?

(January 2019)

A LOOK BACK

MTV launched at 12:01 a.m. on August 1, 1981. The first music video the channel played was the Buggles' video for their 18-month-old #40 hit, "Video Killed the Radio Star," which threw down the gauntlet, proclaiming that a new era was being born and the traditional medium of choice for listening to music—radio—was on its way out.

But that really never came to pass; in fact, just the opposite seemed to have happened. Chris Feldman, author of *The Billboard Book of #2 Singles,* suggests that videos actually boosted radio. He states, "After several down years in the music industry in the early 1980s, MTV offered people what were essentially 'four-minute commercials' for new music that they may never have known about, prompting them to request those songs from the radio stations and ask for them in their local record stores. The 'British Invasion' of the 1980s, led by visual bands like Duran Duran and Culture Club, was largely prompted because people saw those acts and their videos on MTV."

A great example of the effect of music video at that time was Michael Jackson's album *Thriller.* Released in late November of 1982, and previewed by the Paul McCartney duet "The Girl Is

Mine," which had no music video but nonetheless hit #2 on the pop chart, the album sold steadily, but couldn't overcome Men at Work's *Business As Usual* to top the album charts its first couple months of release. That moment finally came in February 1983, as Michael's hit "Billie Jean," powered by its iconic music video, started a seven-week run at #1. That song pushed the album to the top of the sales chart as well, where it stayed for the next three months, as Michael's follow-up single "Beat It" (also accompanied by a memorable video) also hit #1 and the *Motown 25* TV special kept Michael and his moonwalk in front of potential music buyers. For the last half of 1983, although the album occasionally returned to #1 for a week here and there as Michael kept hitting the Top 10 with songs like "Human Nature" and "P.Y.T. (Pretty Young Thing)," which didn't have music videos, most of that time the best-selling albums belonged to the Police, Quiet Riot, and Lionel Richie. In early December, however, Michael released his epic 14-minute video for the song "Thriller." Although the song itself only reached #4, the album (which by that point had been out for over a year) jumped back to #1 on the album chart at the end of December and stayed as the best-selling album each week until mid-April of 1984. As there were no other singles released from the album (in fact, Michael was topping the charts at that time with another Paul McCartney duet, "Say Say Say," that didn't even appear on *Thriller*), it seemed the prime driver of the renewed interest in the album was the release of that video, giving Michael his seventh Top 10 hit from the album. That suggests that, rather than killing the radio star, video helped revive the radio star—prior to *Thriller,* only five albums (two of them soundtracks) had ever generated four Top 10 hits. During the video-rich 1980s alone, 36 albums accomplished that feat, from acts such as Lionel Richie,

Finding that next big hit in the current age involves much more than just relying on radio to guide the way.

Bruce Springsteen, Prince, Madonna, George Michael, Milli Vanilli, Bobby Brown, Debbie Gibson, Richard Marx, Paula Abdul, Expose, Whitney Houston, Genesis (and Phil Collins, solo), Janet Jackson, Heart, Huey Lewis and the News, New Kids on the Block, Chicago, and Miami Sound Machine, among others.

TODAY

If music video failed to fulfill the bold prophecy that the Buggles predicted and make it a reality, the digital age may have done the job. In a report cited by an August 2017 issue of *Variety* magazine, the future of radio as a main source of discovering new music for the public may be bleak. "AM/FM radio is in the midst of a massive drop-off as a music-discovery tool by younger generations, with self-reported listening to AM/FM radio among

47

teens aged 13 and up declining by almost 50 percentage points between 2005 and 2016," according to a report published by New York University's Steinhart Music Business Program. "Generation Z (those born after 1995), which is projected to account for 40% of all consumers in the U.S. by 2020, shows little interest in traditional media, including radio, having grown up in an on-demand digital environment." The survey found that digital platforms such as YouTube, Spotify, and Pandora Radio are now the mediums of choice where Generation Z and others go to discover new music.

Adding to radio's woes is the fact that "By 2020, 75% of new cars are expected to be 'connected' to digital services, breaking radio's monopoly on the car dashboard and relegating AM/FM to just one of a series of audio options behind the wheel."

Of course, since the inception of the Mobile DJ as an entertainment option, DJs have often depended on radio and maybe the Billboard charts to help guide them to what would be the latest big dance floor packer at their next event. That has gotten increasingly more difficult given the multitude of listening options that today's listeners have. In the DJ world, however, radio doesn't always go hand-in-hand with what packs the dance floor. Songs like ZZ Top's "Sharp Dressed Man," the Romantics' "What I Like About You," and line dances like the Cha-Cha Slide, the Cupid Shuffle, and the Electric Slide never reached Top 40 status. A song like Clarence Carter's "Strokin'," which for a time was certain to pack the dance floor, received almost no radio airplay because of its suggestive lyrics. But people had to have found out about it from somewhere. If not radio, where? In those cases, the answer was often other dances where the song was played.

WHAT TO DO

So, if not radio, where are people discovering these new songs? Chris Feldman, who admits he rarely listens to traditional radio stations anymore, says he finds new music from various sources. "I learned about 'Gangnam Style' from a *Saturday Night Live* sketch, and I heard a couple recent favorites from the show's musical acts. I learned about Rebecca Black's 'Friday' because people on Facebook were discussing how annoying it was. I discovered Ariana Grande's 'Thank U, Next' from a Yahoo article that mentioned how she name dropped her ex's in it. And every so often I'll scan the Billboard Top 20, since that's largely sales and streaming driven, and check those songs out on YouTube to stay up on what's popular. The last liked song I remember discovering from the radio was Brandy Clarke's 'Girl Next Door,' which I heard while getting a haircut. But as for how those songs that reach the pop chart initially get discovered? That's probably a question for someone younger than me."

The way I see it, finding that next big hit in the current age involves much more than just relying on radio to guide the way.

It practically requires watching social media, news articles, iTunes and Amazon sales charts for digital music, TV, screening new requests at events, and so many other ways to see if a trend begins to appear. It may be the best way to find the dance floor favorites in the new year.

Chapter 11

Following Through

(December 2013)   Advertisements constantly promise us sure ways to bring more customers to our doorstep, whether it's through driving more people to our website, suggesting more effective ways to network, providing advice on how to "get the client meeting," or suggesting ways to close a sale.

These tips are all great to help you book more events, but then what? What about the next step, or what I like to call Part 2 of the experience, that period between closing the sale and the actual event? From my perspective, it seems like the DJ industry standard is to reel the customer in with persuasive advertising and marketing, meet with the client, close the sale, . . . and then say, "Thank you very much. I'll be in touch with you three or four weeks before your event," even though that event may be nearly a year or more away.

"They [other DJs] spend so much time chasing the customer, and when they get them, they go and chase more," says Scott Faver, owner of The Party Favers in Phoenix, Arizona, emphasizing the fact that the newly signed client is, for the most part, forgotten about from the moment he or she signs on the dotted line until just weeks before the celebration.

Scott takes a different approach: He keeps in contact with his upcoming clients through a series of e-mail tips and meets with them up to four times before the actual performance date arrives.

"My customers are so excited about my follow up and my follow through—that I continue to show that I care about them and their event even before I've done the performance—that they're already starting to refer me to family and friends, their bridesmaids, their parents that are having an anniversary . . . even before their event has taken place," says Scott.

Ron Ruth of Ron Ruth Wedding Entertainment in Kansas City, Missouri, echoes those same sentiments. "I try to schedule an evening with the client just to talk with them about *them*," Ron explains. "We usually do it over the dinner hour and I buy the pizza. You wouldn't believe how much you can learn about a couple while having pizza with them."

This initial meeting takes place months before the client's event. In fact, Ron meets with his clients several times before their actual wedding day. And even though that first meeting may not be until three months before their "big day," by then he has already touched base with them a time or two via e-mail just to inquire how plans are going and offer any help. His first meeting, the "Pizza meeting," is where he gets to know the couple on a more personal level, followed a month later with the actual planning meeting and concluding with a final meeting about 30 days before the event at their venue to get a visual of where and how everything will be laid out—and work out. He even attends the wedding rehearsal, whether he is involved in providing services for that part of their day or not, just for the opportunity to meet the wedding party and walk through the following day's itinerary.

"It's all about relationship building," says Ron.

"The fortune is in the follow-up. Those with a process profit."—Scott Faver

Keeping in touch is a great way to fortify those ties. Stephanie Padovani of Book More Brides adds, "This really strengthens your relationship, creates trust and lets them know you care. It's also a good way to address any issues early on, such as picking out special songs or dealing with difficult parent requests. Then both of you can avoid dealing with the stress later on.

"I've had brides who would literally e-mail me at least once a week with questions before the wedding!" Stephanie continues. "That was overkill, but by the time the wedding arrived we really knew each other, and they knew without a doubt they could rely on me."

Scott couldn't agree more; in fact, he believes to do otherwise is detrimental to your business in the long run.

"If you are slow in answering their e-mails, if you don't return their phone calls, if you show no interest [in keeping in touch], because you're too busy chasing the next deposit, they're not going to come back to you because their experience with you up to the point of the performance—no matter how great that is—did not go over well."

Scott recommends building an electronic database by using a Customer Resource Management software program such as DJ Manager, DJ Event Planner, or Gigbuilder to keep in touch with your clients before, during, and after their momentous moment.

"Your database is like your garden, and you have to tend to your garden," advises Scott. "You're weeding out those who bounce on you, you are adding new names to your list and you are taking care of those that are on your list."

Wedding marketing expert Rick Brewer, owner of GetMoreBrides.com, advises that the time from taking the deposit check to the bank until the time before that first meeting can be spent a couple of different ways to enhance your customer service. "If she [the bride] gets something she's not expecting, you've earned her trust," he says. That something unexpected could be a helpful wedding tip or something as simple as an e-mail inquiring how things are going and offering any assistance. Another customer service tip Rick suggests is asking your clients who their other vendors are and contacting them to go over details, thus "creating peace of mind, better execution and knowing that we are all hitting on all cylinders."

But Rick confesses, "We're not trying to facilitate meetings here, we're trying to create more business," which will be the result of more referrals from happy customers who have been impressed with your willingness to unexpectedly go the extra mile. And the way I see it, that is what customer service is all about anyway.

The added bonus of this extra attention is an event that will run smoother. "If you prepare you shall not fear," says Rick. "When we show up prepared it makes our events so much easier—and fun!"

"The fortune is in the follow-up," Scott likes to say. "Those with a process profit. Constant contact is being bugged, quality content of value is being loved!"

Chapter 12

Has the Needle Moved?

Author's Note: In the early days of 2017 I read a report detailing the average costs of weddings for the previous year. I was disheartened to see the wedding DJs were near the bottom of that list per cost.

"How can this be?" I asked myself. Thus started my quest. What was to be fodder for an article turned into a three-part series spanning March to May of that year. I talked to many of the industry leaders and garnered great input. Truthfully, I thought it was my best work as a writer, but the series received little attention—or at least not much feedback. However, I think it does raise some important question for our industry.

Part 1

(March 2017) In 2015, at the now-leveled Riviera Hotel in Las Vegas, Nevada, Mark Ferrell was about to re-emerge on the Mobile DJ scene as part of the 19th Annual Mobile Beat Las Vegas Show. His entrance, with music blaring, lights flashing, and an entourage parading in front of him, resembled something from Elvis Presley's Vegas heyday. Yes, Mark knew how to capture people's attention. He was back and ready to inspire a group that had seemingly grown uninspired.

A BRIEF HISTORY

In 1998, Mark Ferrell took the Mobile DJ industry by storm by unveiling his "Getting What You're Worth" seminar. In an age when most in the business were making $500 or less per event, Mark was advocating that the minimum standard should be at least $1,200 for each of those gigs. "People pay more for the veggie platters!" he was known to say. The Movement, as it came to be known, was embraced by some, vilified by others, but was without a doubt revolutionary. Many of those who have gone on to substantially raise their fees in this business now reference that movement as the turning point.

"Monumental" is how well-known DJ and author (*Sales for Event Pros*) Mitch Taylor describes it. "The summer of 2000 was when I first saw Mark and whether people admit it or not it (the "Getting What You're Worth" movement) was absolutely, unequivocally monumental." Mitch went on to attend many of Mark's workshops and credits him for giving him the direction that has been a huge part of his success. Bill Hermann, creator of the Entertainment Experience Workshop and a former co-host of the Mobile Beat Show, described the "Get What You're Worth" movement as life-changing for him as he introduced Mark Ferrell for that 2015 seminar: "I personally went from $350 to $1,200 overnight," said Bill.

Mark himself described the "Getting What You're Worth" movement this way: "For one time in the Mobile DJ industry, DJs united. They all came together from 2001 to 2003 and joined associations and formed associations and collaborated and raised prices and prices doubled in less than two years, and nothing has happened like that since."

Now Mark was back, ready to once again reignite the base. He talked about red pills and blue pills, the metaphor made famous by the motion picture *The Matrix*. As described in a Wikipedia entry on the phenomenon: "*The **red pill** and its opposite, the **blue pill,** are popular culture symbols representing the choice between embracing the sometimes painful truth of reality (red pill) and the blissful ignorance of illusion (blue pill).*" Mark asked the gathering of DJs who they thought they were, or, better yet, who we thought WE were as an industry. Perception is a reality, he explained, and our perception is what the public sees and expects. He implored us to once again unite. "We need to come together. We need one overarching non-profit national trade association with leadership that changes, board members that make decisions, a membership who participates in those decisions," he argued. Clowns are more organized than DJs, he lectured. He then invited those who wanted to take leadership in those principles to join him on stage.

"If your reason for leadership is to serve others, stand up," he implored. "If your reason for leadership is to make the world a better place, stand up. If your reason for leadership is to bring people together, to change public perception, to tell the truth and take the high road, to create meaning and inspire other leaders, do something beneficial and lasting for something that's bigger than yourself, stand up!" Dozens stood and joined him on the stage.

HAS THE NEEDLE MOVED?

Now, the question has to be asked: What has happened since that Come-to-Jesus moment? It's been nearly two years since Mark's speech. Has another movement been born? Has that inspirational seminar inspired a new generation? Has the needle moved in terms of making the Mobile DJ industry a recognized true profession in which someone can make a decent living?

"I don't think as an industry we are even ready to talk about whether we've moved needles because there are no statistics to back it up and with no statistical evidence who's to say?" says well-known wedding DJ and creator of the Audiomazing Love Story, Ron Ruth. "I know with my business personally, and with other DJs that I know, we have substantially moved the needle in our own businesses. Does that do anything to move the needle in the industry? I have no idea."

In the days that followed that rallying cry in Vegas a new entity was born—The International Disc Jockey News Academy (IDJNA), an in-depth training and certification program that includes some of the best in our industry to help Mobile DJs improve in all areas of their business. In addition, Mark Ferrell began The Red Pill Movement Facebook page. But the effectiveness of either of those has to be debated. To date, fewer than 100 have joined Mark's Facebook group and even fewer have pursued the training of the IDJNA. Although *Mobile Beat* magazine published an article, "State of the Industry" (January 2017), which indicated 68% of the nearly 1,300 respondents answered they had seen their revenue grow in 2016, a more complete survey by The Wedding Report, long considered the authority in wedding costs throughout the country, revealed that the average amount couples paid for a DJ for their wedding this past year was only $735, a far cry less than the $1,200 benchmark that Mark Ferrell proposed NEARLY 20 YEARS AGO, and was only approximately 3% of a couple's average wedding budget.

"There's a ton of people not charging a whole lot of money to make their efforts count."—Jake Riniker

So where did that group go, those who stood on the stage with Mark at the Riviera in 2015 and pledged to be the next generation of leaders to help bring the Mobile DJ community together? It's not certain, but some of those in attendance may have went out for a race.

A RACE TO THE BOTTOM

In an article posted by Mike Fernino, administrator of the DJ Idea Facebook Group, titled "The Race to the Bottom," Mike questions the logic of the DJ industry. It is, he says, "one of the only industries I know where the participants go out of their way to make less money than a competitor. How is this logical?" A DJ with no training or skills can only compete on price, he surmises, but then counsels "a client who is looking for the lowest bidder does not value you at all."

JAKE'S STORY

One might think Jake Riniker, owner of Riniker Rhythm in southwest Wisconsin, may be the type of DJ Mike is talking about. Jake readily admits he has never been to any type of DJ conference. "I just have not had the opportunity because of other things going on," he says. "But I do believe I'm very keen on what's going on [in the industry]." He also confesses that he has no idea who Mitch Taylor or Bill Hermann are, but he has heard something of Peter Merry and is somewhat familiar with Mark Ferrell ("the Veggie Platter guy, right?"). He doesn't subscribe to any publications and is not part of any Facebook groups, but says he does follow Mobile Beat on Twitter. You might think Jake is one of those $500, bottom feeding part-time DJs you need to compete against. But no, Jake is actually the price trend setter in his area, getting more than double of what The Wedding Report cites as the national average for a wedding reception DJ despite being in the rural community of Platteville, Wisconsin, population 11,000. With such a lack of being "in the loop," so to speak, how is it, then, that he can achieve such a higher-than-average price?

"I'm not afraid to take a risk," he simply states. "There's a ton of people not charging a whole lot of money to make their efforts count. We're considered a hobby, and whether we like it or not that's what people who are not performing the work look at us as. For a lot of industries there are standards and regulations to make sure that the work is done correctly," Jake says. Those standards are absent in the DJ industry. "There's a vast amount of DJs that don't treat this as a profession.

"It's very difficult to up that price point because of the unknown," Jake explains. "Every time I've raised my rates it has been an extremely tough decision. Not being aggressive enough, not seeing the real value that you have, whether that is your company or as an individual" is the roadblock that DJs fail to overcome, Jake surmises.

The way I see it, there is still more to discuss, and we'll do that in Part 2 next month.

The Needle: Part 2

(April 2017)

Why?

That is a question Bill Hermann, former president of the now defunct Minnesota Association of Professional Disc Jockeys, reminds people taking part in his seminars to ask often. As he puts it, "We always ask who, what, where, when, but we seldom ask why."

Why then do DJs average less per event than many of the other wedding professionals—such as photographers, videographers, and coordinators? According to year-end data posted by The Wedding Report, DJs average only $735 per event. Why is the Mobile DJ the Rodney Dangerfield ("I get no respect") of the wedding industry?

It's a frustration that Peter Merry, former president of the American Disc Jockey Association (ADJA) and author of *The Best Wedding Reception . . . Ever!* has experienced for years.

A HUGE TASK

"I think the vast majority of DJs have such a low opinion of what their job is and how easy they think their job is to do that they don't see the value of creating any kind of standards other than you should be using pro tools," Peter said in a recent interview. "When you put the words *work hard* in front of most Mobile DJs it scares them because this is something most do on the side, on their weekends. They don't see it as a real business, a real profession."

During his two years as president of the ADJA, Peter visited over three dozen cities across the United States trying to give Mobile DJs valuable information to strengthen their business as well as encourage them to join the organization. During that time, ADJA membership grew to approximately 1,200 members. That number may be relatively low, however, considering that the estimated number of people calling themselves Mobile DJs may exceed 75,000 nationally. Peter's tour, along with Mark Ferrell's "Getting What You're Worth" movement during the preceding years, helped prices increase for the Mobile DJ industry. But then things stagnated. "The fact that the ADJA has never gotten above 2,000 members says a lot about our industry," says Peter.

The problem, as Peter sees it, is twofold. First is the lack of DJs who are willing to educate today's bride. "If the DJ responds to the bride with a price, and doesn't do anything to educate the bride about the VALUE that they'll be receiving [for that price] then the bride is actually being short-changed because then she thinks she can find whoever is cheapest and that guy will do a great job." Second is public perception. "The wedding media . . . is still painting [DJs] as just the music guy who stands in the corner until it's time to cut the cake."

It's for those reasons that Peter never quotes a price until he has had an opportunity to speak with a future bride. "If they're willing to have a conversation, we'll talk, and by the time we're done—even if she doesn't hire me—she'll probably spend twice as much as she originally budgeted because she knows what to look for now."

You would think that, in an age in which Mobile DJs are nearly as much a part of a wedding celebration as the white dress, the general public would recognize DJs for their talents and creativity, but are most Mobile DJs creators or just imitators?

CREATIVITY AND THE DIGITAL AGE

"I believe that DJs are in one of the most creative industries on the planet," says four-time Wedding MBA presenter Ron Ruth. "Therefore, I would expect that DJs would be creative thinkers. Unfortunately, I believe there is a breed of DJs entering our industry who are focused more on making a few bucks than they are in generally making a positive impact on peoples' lives or exercising their creative muscles.

"I believe that the countless conduits of information that have been popping up in every social media stream, from Facebook groups to podcasts, are actually counterproductive. Instead of advancing the concept of DJs first relying on their own imagination and creative skills, those social outlets are encouraging their audience to blindly imitate the information being disseminated by individuals who may or may not be giving accurate information that may or may not be appropriate in every situation. Creativity is about taking risks. Individuals who refuse to take risks of their own should not be confused with true creative thinkers and innovators."

"I believe that DJs are in one of the most creative industries on the planet." —Ron Ruth

For all of the wonders the digital age has brought us, it has had a negative impact on many industries, such as music stores, advertising, and print publications. Its effect can be felt on the DJ industry as well.

"Everything is supposed to be free now. If you want information you'll find a YouTube video to teach you," says Michael Buonaccorso, author of *A Different Spin: The DJ Story.* "The value of education has just rapidly dropped. I can't see that the digital age has done anything other than make it easier to do anything. Now the only thing you can offer is personality. There was a time when your music collection counted for something. Now that asset doesn't exist."

Michael has been around long enough to know. By 1990 he had already been a Mobile DJ for several years when he and his business partner, Bob Lindquist, decided that the fledgling DJ industry needed a platform, so they created *Mobile Beat* magazine in 1991. Over the next 25 years, Michael saw up close an evolving industry, one that would alternately progress and regress. He's seen movements and organizational attempts come and go time after time.

"Some of the people that were asking the questions years ago sort of faded away," said Michael. "I've seen things go almost around in cycles. It seems like every five years these things come around and no one quite understands what happens." Years later, a new enthused group of DJs emerge. "It's like a Ferris wheel," he said. "There's never been anything to sustain a base. Any organization of any individuals has to have some structure in place that makes it possible to exist but the Mobile DJs never got to that point."

As for industry leaders, Michael questions if that is even a term we should be using.

"The people that we call leaders are not really leading anything. What are they leading? Do they have people that report to them? If you wrote a book and gave a seminar and the room is full you're not leading those people—you're talking to them.

"A lot of people have given me credit over the years for being a 'leader' by the very fact that I gave them a vehicle [the magazine], but I wasn't the driver, I just owned the car."

The same can be said for "movements.

"When you call these things a 'movement' it's really just an idea that you heard from somebody and thought it sounded good. There wasn't a place to say 'Sign me up, I'm going to do this, I'm going to attend this meeting, I'm going to pay my dues.' Like in 1998 when Mark Ferrell walked into a room full of guys with cut off shorts and stupid t-shirts and said 'Listen guys, wake up!' [He had] great ideas and inspiration, but he couldn't force anyone to change anything. Some did, while others resented (and still do) that he brought up the subject."

Lack of leadership, lack of organization, lack of structure, and a naive public: does that all add up to $735?

The way I see it, as part of that least-paid community of wedding vendors, we may be still asleep.

I'll wrap this all up next month.

A Brief Summary

The Wedding Report	2016
Wedding Dress/es	$1,221
Live Band	$1,695
Engagement Ring	$3,407
Wedding Bands	$1,242
Wedding Photographer	$1,611
Wedding Videographer	$1,072
Wedding Coordinator	
-Day of	$812
-For Getting Started	$875
. -Full Service	$2,773
-Month of Direction	$1,062
DJ	$735

Adapted from data provided by WeddingReport.com, 2016.

The Needle: Part 3

(May 2017)

A FEW GOOD MEN

Peter Merry and Mark Ferrell are just two of the names that have stepped forward for the cause of the Mobile DJ. After two years on the road, though, Peter had to return to his "normal" life and take care of business. "I probably lost $30,000 in bookings during that time," he said.

Ron Ruth has been a presenter at the Wedding MBA for the past four years, and is preparing to do so again this fall. The airfare and the hotel costs are almost always on his own dime. Why does he do it?

"I love inspiring people," he says. "I'm not going to tell you how to do whatever it is that you do, but rather hope you find the inspiration to do it yourself."

For Mitch Taylor, it is now a daily occurrence to get to the office early to do a morning Facebook video broadcast, "#Live at 755," before his work day begins. That is not always an easy task when you live in Escanaba, Michigan, where it is not uncommon to have temperatures below zero on those January or February mornings. Why does he do it?

"For me it's a way to give back to an industry that has given me so much," he says. "Live" is just one of the ways Mitch gives back. He also co-administers a Facebook page, Sales for Event Pros; helps critique and advise fellow DJs, many times free of charge; and has also done many speaking engagements pro bono.

"We're in the midst of a changing industry, and how we consume information is changing. Where that is going we just don't know."—John Young

You can add John Young to the list as well. As publisher of *Disc Jockey News,* John has traveled from coast to coast attending any type of an expo or conference in an effort to give the industry updated and relevant information. Couple that with days that start at 8 a.m. and don't end sometimes until after 10 p.m. when he wraps up another episode for DJN-TV, and it's a heavy load. Why take on such a burdensome endeavor? "It began in an effort to help DJs be better business people," says John.

I could add at least another two dozen men—and women—to the list who have given freely of their time and talents to help advance the industry to be recognized as a true, reputable career choice.

THE OTHER VIEW

Not everyone feels that way, though. Comments I have heard as I undertook this project were evident of that.

"I've been deejaying for eight years. What are they going to tell me at a conference that I don't already know?" was one response I received from a local DJ when asked why he had no interest in attending a conference.

"I don't understand why DJs get worked up about so called 'bottom feeders' or the image of the industry," was another I received through a Facebook post.

"I am not concerned about the 'we.' I am only concerned about the 'me' when it comes to getting paid," was still another.

The "me" rather than "we" attitude is certainly prevalent among our community, maybe now more so than ever before.

AND A WORD FROM THE PRESIDENT

Hugo Drax, the long-time president of the ADJA, has seen that attitude. The association has long been considered the leading organization of the Mobile DJ community, but a dwindling membership puts that in question. Their website lists 27 chapters "in formation" and only eight as active, with half of those located in the western part of the United States. Hugo has seen the issues facing the community but is not entirely sold on the premise that it is caused by so much free content that is so available with today's technology.

"Content doesn't impact the pricing in the market; bad business impacts the price of the market," he states.

"How many pictures do we see of DJ's who have sloppy set ups? We see pictures of them sitting. We see pictures of them eating. We have these images that we've pro-generated ourselves.

"People only want to pay for something they perceive has value. In the absence of value everybody shops on price."

And he adds, "The industry is never going to move as long as the overwhelming majority do this as a hobby."

MY FINAL THOUGHTS

As DJs, is it reasonable to think we should be considered any more of a legitimate business than the person who sells Tupperware or Avon products? True, more men and women than ever before are making a living as a Mobile DJ, but even though that number has grown one wonders how many of those operate their business as a "real" business? How many have a store front or have their employees classified as employees, with taxes taken out of their checks and covered with liability insurance as opposed to being classified as a subcontractor? How many have sought out the advice from the Small Business Development Center, and then followed it? How many have a business plan? What percentage invest in any type of further education, other than what they find on social media? Why would we expect the public to think any more of us when we do not hold ourselves to the same standards that we would expect? The way I see it I have found the enemy . . . and the enemy is us.

FAVORITE LINES

I'll wrap this up with my favorite quotes I've heard while putting this series together:

"I don't think DJs should be concerning themselves with what everyone else is doing and focus on what they're doing. If they can move the needle within their own business that's quite an accomplishment."—Ron Ruth

"In the end, and I don't know if it will move the needle, but people have to be motivated to improve themselves."—Hugo Drax

"I think John Young has done amazing things with what he's done with *Disc Jockey News* and where that's grown over the last two years. I'm just not convinced of any other entity right now being able to really be the voice that DJs need at this time. I think that technology has squeezed some people, forcing the talent to rise to the top and it's forcing people to evolve. And those that don't want to evolve and stay where they are at are going to perish."—Mitch Taylor

"We're in the midst of a changing industry, and how we consume information is changing. Where that is going we just don't know."—John Young

SECTION III
Personal Experiences

Chapter 13

Misfortune Turns to Good Fortune

(September 2012) It started out like any other wedding day. I set up earlier in the day, arrived back 30 minutes before my scheduled time, and ran through my checklist. As the guests started to arrive I began to play some of that toe tapping background music. About 30 minutes into the reception someone popped in to tell me that the wedding party was on-site, so I put on a nice long song, announced to the guests that the wedding party had arrived, and went out to meet with them and get prepped for introductions. Once out in the hallway, I encountered a couple of wedding party members, but no bride and groom. I was told they were checking into their hotel room and would be arriving shortly. Several minutes later I stepped back into the banquet room to discover several guests with cameras ready, eagerly awaiting the arrival of the bride and groom. I announced that "Tanya and Wayne" were still taking care of some business and would be joining us shortly. However, despite several more trips to the hall over the next several minutes, there was still no bride and groom. By this time the guests had returned to their seats. Finally, I peeked down the hall further and noticed a commotion by the men's restroom. I made my way there to see what was going on and discovered a few of the groomsmen, the bride, and her mother all gathered *in the*

79

men's restroom with the groom sprawled out on the floor. He had just gotten sick on himself and appeared very intoxicated. I returned to the banquet room and let the guests know that the groom was feeling ill and we were getting him some attention; however, by this time word of what had happened was already spreading through the reception. The minister who had performed the ceremony came and spoke with me and assured me that there was no alcohol on anyone's breath during the ceremony. Moments later, the groom's uncle, a paramedic, was summoned for help.

"Call 911," he said. "This guy has alcohol poisoning,"

Success often comes with the help of others. Don't be afraid to depend on that.

It seems in their quest to celebrate the moment, the wedding party bar-hopped from the ceremony to the reception and the groomsmen kept buying the groom shots—even though the groom was no drinker. As a result, one of the enduring images of the couple's wedding day was Wayne being carted out of the hall on a stretcher.

But this is where the story took an interesting turn. The families decided to go ahead with dinner, and I anticipated the reception would come to a quiet close after that. But I continued my usual routine and began ramping up the music a bit at the conclusion of dessert. To my surprise, two young ladies came to the floor and began to dance. A song or two later several others joined them. I took a moment to approach my first two dancers and quizzed them on what songs they thought might work best there. They revealed to me that Tanya and a large group of her friends went country line dancing every Wednesday night (funny that never came up at the consultation), so I had something to start with. In just a song or two the dance floor was packed! Then someone received a phone call: The bride was on her way back. When she arrived we were ready for her. As she came through the door, I announced, "Ladies and gentleman, the bride is in the house!" and went right into Nick Lowe's "I Knew the Bride (When She Used to Rock and Roll)." My two unanticipated assistants grabbed her, pulled her onto the dance floor, and the party was on.

We did the father/daughter dance and the dollar dance. At one point, a pair of her bridesmaids pulled her to the floor, forced her into a chair, ripped off her garter, and threw it. We followed that with the bouquet toss. With only an hour or so left in the reception, the groom appeared, came just inside the door, and waved to everyone, just to let them know that he was okay. He disappeared down the hall and the bride followed him. Things began to wind down after that, but the minister and several others approached me to tell me what an unbelievable job I had done and could not believe how things had turned out.

But I knew it was not only me. I searched out my two early dancers and asked them to step out into the hallway.

"You two," I told them, "are as responsible as anyone to turn what could have been a tragic day into a terrific one. Go to sleep tonight knowing you are good people!"

With tears in their eyes, they said they had to do it for Tanya. Within days the phone started ringing from others at their wedding that were planning an event and were so impressed how everything had turned out that they wanted to meet with me. But I knew a lot of the credit had to go to my two helpful ladies.

The way I see it, there were a couple lessons to learn from that celebration. One was that Yogi Berra was right, "It ain't over 'til it's over." Keep looking for that spark that will ignite a fire. The other is that success often comes with the help of others. Don't be afraid to depend on that.

Chapter 14

It's the Secret Ingredient

(July 2013) I can still see him, peering over his glasses as he looked through my brochures and business synopsis. After a prolonged, uncomfortable silence he finally spoke.

"So you want to be a hot shot DJ?" he asked.

"Well, I'm not sure I want to be a hot shot," I countered and then explained to him that, after 15 years of being a part-time DJ, I was ready to try to make it as a full-time entertainer.

"Why would you want to leave [your current employment] after 15 years to pursue THIS?" he inquired.

"Because this is my passion," I confessed to him. "This is what I love to do."

"WRONG ANSWER!" he stated.

So I took a second attempt. "Well, I've maxed out as far as I will go in my current employment," I explained of my job at a family run weekly newspaper. "I just think I have much more potential here."

"WRONG ANSWER!" he stated again, emphatically.

After a couple of more attempts I gave up.

"Then I guess I don't know what the right answer is," I confessed.

And he put it to me simply: "To make money! That is the only reason to be in business."

The man's name was Terry and he was a representative of the Small Business Development Center, a government agency designed to provide a vast array of technical assistance to small businesses and aspiring entrepreneurs. And over our next three or four sessions, he taught me a lot on what is necessary to sustain a successful business. There are great mechanics, wonderful cooks, and fantastic photographers, he noted, but that does not make them great business owners. Now in my fifth year of being the full-time owner and operator of this mom-and-pop shop I call Alexxus Entertainment, I understand what he was telling me. And I've learned a lot along the way. I've learned first and foremost that owning your own business is not much different than farming, because you are never finished. There is always something more that needs to be done. I've also discovered that balancing your commitments between work, family, and home projects is a never ending struggle.

But of all the things I've learned, there is something I mentioned to him when we first met that I still believe is the cornerstone of which a small business is built on, and that is passion. Now that I have had the opportunity to be around so many other entrepreneurs over the past five years, I find that to be the common denominator among those that have been truly successful. "There is joy in work. There is no happiness except in the realization that we have accomplished something," Henry Ford once said. And true enough, the way I see it, those that have been most giving of themselves look to be the ones that go the furthest.

I've always believed that talent will only take you so far, and intelligence will only take you so far, but drive and perseverance is what takes you over the top.

In the Mobile DJ industry, it seems evident to me that those with a passion are those that thrive. I see it in John Young, publisher of the *Disc Jockey News,* as he criss-crosses the country attending expos and seminars to promote the paper to potential advertisers. I hear it in Mitch Taylor's voice when he answers a

I've always believed that talent will only take you so far, and intelligence will only take you so far, but drive and perseverance is what takes you over the top.

phone call from a potential client, or when he has to cancel dinner plans in Vegas just because duty calls, or watching Ken Day and Ed Spencer compare the apps they have discovered on their new electronic devices in a hotel room in Minnesota (how do you weight your sound?). It's in every one of Brian Kelm's social networking posts and Brian Redd's videos, and so obvious in Peter Merry, who not only strives to continually improve himself but to see the DJ industry—particularly the wedding DJ—be better as a whole from coast to coast. It is plain as the nose on your face in my conversations with Ron Ruth In my 20-plus years as a part-time-turned-full-time DJ, I have seen many come and go in the wedding profession. Some blame economics, others reason it's because of the attitudes of the customers they've had to deal with. Or some simply exit because they set their price point too low and did not have enough capital to reinvest in their business when new technology came along or when doing a pair of bridal shows and placing an ad in the Yellow Pages was no longer the answer for marketing. But what I really have seen in those that call it quits was the loss of their passion.

Not long ago, that was me. I began to feel our weddings were reruns. I was struggling to motivate myself to get out of my office chair and network. But in a span of six months I attended a pair of DJ-related conventions and participated in a business core strengthening program through our local Chamber of Commerce. Nothing reinvigorates you like being around successful individuals and sharing ideas.

If your passion has begun to wane, if you've ever asked yourself what do you need to do to get more leads, to close more deals, to up your price, then I suggest you attend one of the many DJ conventions or conferences that are out there, that you participate in one of the DJ-designed workshops that are available, or at the very least take advantage of the educational opportunities in your local area, join a networking group, or even buy and read a business-related book. I can't think of anyone who has undertaken those activities and felt it was a waste of their time and money.

Chapter 15

Expectations of the Mobile DJ Grow

(October 2015) On a late summer afternoon last month I prepared for my 36th wedding of the year—an outdoor event on a hill overlooking the mighty Mississippi River. I had set up my equipment earlier in the morning, but returned in plenty of time to go through my final checklist. Moments after I returned, wedding guests began to pop in even though, according to my planner sheet, they were not due for another hour. Nonetheless, I put on some background music to create a little ambience under the tent and continued with my preparations. The early arriving guests were followed by a videographer who had barely been there a couple minutes before he asked if he could tap into my sound system for his audio—and if I had the right connections to accommodate that request. While trying to satisfy the videographer's needs, the wedding party arrived and sent notice that they were ready to be introduced . . . 30 minutes ahead of schedule. In a matter of minutes, the photographers and I had them lined up and introduced them all. Then they took it upon themselves to be seated for dinner—even though we were still a half hour ahead of schedule. While preferable to being a half hour behind schedule, it does present some other challenges. Before handing over the microphone to this couple for the traditional blessing before

dinner, I checked in with the catering staff to see if they could accommodate an earlier meal time; they asked me to give them five minutes and they would be ready. As I continued through my preshow checklist, I noticed that there was no cake topper or knife and server at the cake table. I informed a personal attendant and she immediately went in search of the missing items.

As I approached the head table with the microphone, I was pulled to the side by a bridesmaid, given a flash drive, and asked—when toast time arrived—to play a track off of it when cued. I was also asked to supply her with two cordless microphones!

What is expected of Mobile DJs in the 21st century and where do the obligations end?

Early arriving guests, audio connections, flash drives, multiple microphones, and an MIA cake knife? These are things that are never mentioned in pre-event meetings with clients, but expected still the same. The point of this story is not to be considered for an entry for the next edition of the book *Wedding Horror Stories— and How to Avoid Them,* but to raise a question: What is expected of Mobile DJs in the 21st century and where do the obligations end?

This wedding was not just an isolated incident. In the month of September alone:

- We were asked to play an obscure song (several times). When we informed the guest that we did not have that track, we were asked to "YouTube it." We even had one guest return with $2.00 to pay to have the track downloaded. We did find it and played it.

- Another wedding party member approached us with a CD that apparently contained a song that her boyfriend had written and recorded for the bride and groom. Unfortunately for this bridesmaid, my associate that handled this wedding used laptops that did not contain a CD drive—and we retired those dual decks a long time ago.

- At another wedding, the father of the bride informed us that the bride's grandfather was lead singer of a band back in his day, so he wondered if we could play a karaoke version of "Route 66" and let him sing it. I have to ask, how many of us carry a karaoke version of "Route 66" at all times? (We were able to make that request happen, however.)

Is this dilemma a product of our overall instant gratification society or the fact that today's millennials have come to expect us to have so many wishes fulfilled at the push of a couple of keystrokes?

Joe Martin, a member of the Disc Jockey Hall of Fame and 40-plus-year veteran of the Mobile DJ industry, may be best able to answer that question.

91

"I have been there, done that," he admits. "As I look back over the last 40 years, I've had many curves thrown my way." One of his upcoming events is a prime example. "I'm doing a school reunion next week and I was informed months after the contract signing that I will be working with a band. I have no problem with that but some might. Some DJs might not care about not playing [the same] songs the band will play," he continues, "but it requires time for me to make sure I don't by reviewing their play list.

"Two weeks before the event I am notified I will need to play a backing track for a rapper. I spend a little time to find the right track and buy it. Then the 'rapper' informs me one week out that I will need to provide three microphones."

Another one of those stories is not his own but one he recently read about on a social media post.

"The DJ gets told at the last minute to change the bride and groom's first dance song to the Gene Vincent cover version of 'You Belong to Me,' a song made popular by other artists. Why they wanted the Vincent version, who knows?

"The DJ has an Internet connection and finds the song on Amazon. He buys the song but does not have time to review it— and the Amazon listing was mismarked! He hits play as the couple makes their way to the floor for their first dance, and out of the speakers comes a twangy rendition of 'Your Cheating Heart'."

Joe continued, "I don't know why I'm still laughing," but uninformed guests and the shocked couple were probably not.

But he concludes, "I'm not so sure that things haven't always been that clients expect us to have a solution for everything. Some expect it at the last minute. Others do give a little notice. I think it boils down to clients and others expect us to be able to handle anything."

Fellow Hall of Famer and longtime Minnesota DJ John Young has seen the problem grow as well and offers this advice:

"I think the expectations come from desperate DJs who will do EVERYTHING or offer to sell EVERYTHING they can think of for a minimum fee."

The way I see it, John may be on to something. By being more detailed with our clients early on, they'll be able to answer when one of their guests approaches them and asks why the DJ won't play a song off of his or her phone or download the last-minute request—and it may also prevent a brand new married couple from dancing to "Your Cheating Heart!" on their wedding day.

Sure we could argue that many of these scenarios are not within our responsibility, but being right and doing the right thing is not always the same thing, but only one of those choices will help you on the road to success.

Chapter 16

You Must Like Me

(November 2013) Sally Field has had a run that would be the envy of almost any performer. Now in her sixth decade as an actress, Sally has earned Emmy, Oscar, and Golden Globe awards for her impressive acting career, both on TV and in film, going back to the 1960s TV sitcom *Gidget.* Yet avid movie fans everywhere will probably remember her best for her 1985 acceptance speech after winning her second Academy Award, when she excitedly exclaimed that now famous phrase, "You like me, you really like me." And although it is not *exactly* what she said (her exact quote was: "I haven't had an orthodox career, and I've wanted more than anything to have your respect. The first time I didn't feel it, but this time I feel it, and I can't deny the fact that you like me, right now, you like me!"), she has probably been remembered and mocked more for that moment than anything she's ever done on film.

However, in that one legendary quote, I feel she said more than several of her predecessors, many of whom gave much longer speeches, simply by what she *did not* say. You see, she did not thank the Academy for recognizing her for her hard work and years of training and studying. She did not feel it was worth mentioning the gratitude they had for her long hours of preparation for her roles. She felt that she was honored because, well, in the end, the Academy really, really liked her.

And more often than not, "being liked" may be the determining factor in many of the decisions that we make, especially in the sales and service field. How many times do we purchase, or have our clients purchase from us, based on comfort and likeability? The way I see it, when all sales pitches are finished, when we've stopped comparing X's and O's, when price is no longer a factor, we generally go with the person that we feel most confident and comfortable with—and that we trust.

In his book *The 29% Solution: 52 Weekly Networking Success Strategies,* co-author and founder of the Business Networkers International Ivan Misner wrote, "People don't care what you know, until they know you care." Maybe then, instead of refining the same sales pitch for each and every customer, we would better serve ourselves if we listened to what that customer wanted first. When I began my DJ business years ago, I would fret over the bookings that I was NOT getting. I felt that if some of these potential customers would just take a chance on me I was certain that they would be more than happy with the product and service that I provided them. Call after call I would explain that I had a comprehensive music library, name brand equipment, and could beat most anyone's price. Yet, unless there was some kind of a friend or family connection, my pleas for their business went unanswered.

I realized that I needed to take a new approach. I started to take more time explaining my services and what a difference I could make at their event. More importantly, I began to ask questions and listened to what each individual client wanted. I made potential customers feel more at ease with me and more confident in me. It was only then that my business began to take off, and price was not always the determining factor.

"People don't care what you know, until they know you care."—Ivan Misner

While it's a good thing to have the latest technology and important to be well educated in your field, in the end I feel my "likeability" probably more so than my gear, music library, or price has had a greater impact on a client's decision to buy, or not to buy, from me than anything else. And, unlike the music and equipment that I utilize, that is not a tool that I can buy in a store or online. It's a constant tweaking and evaluation of oneself.

The way I see it, if I do that well, it's my calendar and bottom line that will scream, "You like me. You really LIKE me!"

Chapter 17

It Pays to Be Nice

Author's Note: This article predates my time writing for the Disc Jockey News, *but I think the message is something that's well worth remembering, so I've chosen to include it here.*

(c. 2011) She was kind of quiet, kept to herself, and, well, she just didn't seem to be one of the popular gals around the building. She worked as a custodian, and I guess you could say she and I were coworkers, although most of my coworkers rarely interacted much with the custodial staff. Nonetheless, whenever she came into my area I was always polite and tried to have a bit of conversation with her.

At that time I was working at a big box printing company, which is where I first met her. A couple of years later, I made some changes in my main career, moving on for better opportunities, and within a year or so I also left my part-time gig at a local multi-op DJ company to venture out as an entertainer on my own.

Just a month or so after making that decision, I was invited to be part of a bridal fair, a rather small event inside a craft store where they were trying to push their wedding accessories. While there making my public debut I saw her, my former coworker. I got her attention and, as it turned out, she remembered me. She was planning to head down the aisle in the near future, with a former classmate of mine no less. I told her how after I left our previous employer I had started my own DJ company. She took my information, and a couple days later called to book me for her event. I had one of my first weddings!

But this story gets better.

The wedding was great. The bride's sister, who served as maid of honor, turned out to be a great facilitator. As the evening wore down, she came by to talk to me and mentioned she had never heard of my company before. I explained to her that I had worked for one of the local multi-ops but just recently started my own entertainment company.

"Well," she replied, "I own a bridal shop. Why don't you bring some of your cards and brochures in and I'll display them in my store?"

"To get lucky—and luck always is in play—you have to get in its path." —Harry Beckwith

As someone looking for work contacts, that sounded great to me. I worked out a business arrangement with her and soon had posters, cards, and brochures available in her bridal shop. In addition, everyone who purchased a wedding dress from her establishment received a $25 gift certificate toward one of my company's services, and I cannot tell you what a boost that was in getting my business off the ground.

Recently I was reminded of this whole scenario by an article I read by author and marketing expert Harry Beckwith, in which he stated, "To get lucky—and luck always is in play—you have to get in its path." I realized that's what I had done. By taking the time to be kind and considerate to this young lady years before, I sowed the seeds of a relationship that helped get me started in a career I didn't even know I'd have back then.

I still see my former coworker from time to time. She now works at a local retail store. When I have the opportunity, I still stop and say hi to her, grateful for the opportunity that she gave me years ago that was instrumental in helping me kick off my business. The way I see it, a smile can go a mile. Being considerate and respectful to most everyone can open up doors down the road you never knew existed.

Chapter 18

Why Are You Here

(May 2016) I can still see Rosemary as she tried to suppress a laugh. We were sitting on a bus, heading to Chicago for a school field trip. Her son and mine were close friends, so we decided to be "bus buddies." What did I say that made her try not to laugh out loud? I mentioned that I was just in Chicago a few weeks earlier for a DJ convention. She almost burst into a hysterical giggle. I didn't press her as to why she found that comment funny, but I could almost read her mind: "What in the world could you learn at a DJ convention?" she must have thought. "Is there a secret to loading a CD player and pushing play? Oh my!"

Now, several years later, while attending the Eighth Annual Midwest DJs (MWDJ) Live Show in Milwaukee, Wisconsin, on April 11th and 12th I remembered this interaction and wished Rosemary was once again sitting next to me. What would she think now if she saw this collection of roughly 150 mobile DJs listening intently to Vickie Musni, who was presenting the second part of her seminar "Color Me Smart"? Most of those in attendance were scribbling notes frantically or taking pictures with their smartphones of the PowerPoint content Vickie displayed on the big screen. What an education Rosemary would herself get if she saw the schooling some DJs actually seek to be a success in this field.

What would she ask these DJs, I wondered, if she were there? My guess is she would probably start with "*Why are you here??*"

Why *ARE* you here? That is a good question, I thought, and I speculated what the answers would be from the attendees that were in the room. So I grabbed my legal pad, wrote "Michael J. Lenstra, *Disc Jockey News*: Why are you here?" across the top, and took it to the end of the row. I asked the group there if they would write their name down, add their company name, and answer that question, then pass the legal pad on. Several of our fellow emcees, entertainers, and DJs were happy to oblige.

The answers were varied but also the same; similar, but different. From the seasoned veterans to the newbies, all gave their take on what drove them to be in attendance for this educational opportunity.

"We are looking to set the standard in the DJ entertainment industry ..." —James Kelley

For longtime DJ Brian Kelm, the quest to keep improving never stops. A veteran of over two dozen workshops within the industry, several more outside (but related to) the industry, and more conferences and conventions than he can count, he was happy to once again attend the MWDJ Live Show for the fourth time. Not only is it just minutes from home, Brian says, but he attends the annual event to "relax and connect with colleagues—and recharge myself with quality content and relationships."

Across the aisle from Brian—and across the spectrum of experience—was Terry Krombos of Hit Entertainment DJs. He was making his first appearance at the show and stated his reason for coming was to "learn more about the business—and networking."

One of the younger attendees to the show was Zaren Nebel of YoDJ Entertainment. His reason for being there? "As the youngest person in the room as a full time DJ I always have so much to learn. This convention has given me so much info and things to put into play over the last two years."

Representing the gender minority was Nicole Young, one of the few females in attendance. Her response to my question: "As a female DJ I'm looking for all the knowledge possible to boost [my] confidence. I'd like to bring as much back to the business as I can to lead me to the highest success possible."

In fact, Corey Young and James Kelley, co-owners of YoDJ Entertainment, had nearly a half dozen of their staff members attend the show and participate in Vickie's workshop the day preceding the event.

Why?

"We are looking to set the standard in the DJ entertainment industry in the Fox Valley, Wisconsin area," explained James.

The way I see it, all of those DJs who left a comment on the yellow legal pad have a common thread, which is to keep improving, to better themselves, and to elevate the industry. Fellow staff writer Jake Palmer, who presented "It's a Conversation, Not a Confrontation" at the show, reminded us that our presence is a great thing, both personally and professionally, but we are only 1% of the Mobile DJ community. We must reach out to the other 99% and inspire them to improve.

But maybe that percentage all think like Rosemary.

SECTION IV:
Final Thoughts

Chapter 19

It's an Age-Old Question

(August 2014) Dave Dunnam of Photographs & Memories in Belmont, Wisconsin, sits patiently in front of his computer screen waiting for the phone to ring while he works on some water-damaged wedding photos for a friend. The phone doesn't ring as much these days.

The reason? Could be the economy. Could be because, as wedding marketing specialist Rick Brewer said in one of his seminars a couple of years ago, "no one has taken it in the shorts more than the photography world" in the new digital age, or it could be something else. Dave, a realist who is on the far back side of 50, thinks he knows what it is: "There comes a point when not too many [high school] seniors or young brides want their picture taken by someone that reminds them of their grandfather anymore."

True enough. There are many professions where the end of the road comes long before it's time to receive your gold watch and start collecting your 401K. Think professional athletes here, or fashion models, or some of Hollywood's biggest and most successful celebrities. After all, has anyone seen Renée Zellweger in a big screen blockbuster lately? Do you think it is her TALENT that has suddenly evaporated?

Does the Mobile DJ profession, or any business in the wedding-related industry for that matter, fall into that category?

In February of this year, newsday.com ran an article about older DJs who were still spinning tunes, albeit at Veterans of Foreign Wars Valentine's Day events or senior living centers. A firestorm of sorts was lit when Hugo Drax, CEO and president of the American Disc Jockey Association, was asked to comment on that. Although he found that admirable, he decreed that, truth be told, Mobile DJ work is indeed an age-limited field. "Being a DJ is really a young man's game," said Hugo. "There's a lot of equipment that comes with it. You're not schlepping records or big books of CDs anymore, but there's still substantial equipment to carry in." Maybe more so than that, he reasoned, "Let's face it, most 26-year-olds don't want 'grandpa' to DJ their wedding."

Some took exception to those words. "I began spinning music at parties in 1979 and have fought age bias my entire career," said one respondent who replied in the comments section of the article and proudly touted himself as a 56-year-old. He then went on to describe more than one instance where clients were super impressed with his performance, even after they discovered his age.

"I am 53 now and still going," said another commenter. "[I] DJ the middle school dances in my town and the kids have a ball! It's all about staying current, enjoying the music and the people, listening to what they like, being personable, professional, and responsible."

I do not doubt that these DJs still do a stellar job, but I think they might have missed the point that Hugo, who according to the article is 57, was trying to make.

At one of his seminars at the Mobile Beat Show in Las Vegas, 1% Solution creator Randy Bartlett, who is also 57, put it this way: "If you were a 27-year-old bride and you're putting a list together of all of the traits that you want from your DJ/Master of Ceremonies—and one of those traits was age—how old do you think they want their DJ/MC to be? What percentage of them would say 57?" Randy goes on to state, "I think the 'sweet spot' age-wise for a wedding DJ is 30–40."

Although he is still busy after 26 years in the business, Randy has seen somewhat of a decline in recent years. "It's difficult to say how much is age-related," said Randy. "I have no doubt that I lose some events because of my age. It's not the only factor, but it's one of many. The wedding I'm doing this weekend came to me through a coordinator who told me they asked her up front how old I was. They hired me sight unseen based on her recommendation, but obviously, age was a concern."

But Randy has a plan.

"My target date for retiring is my 62nd birthday. At that point, I should be completely debt-free," he says. "I know we plan to travel a lot. My wife is already retired. I may still do some events

111

from time to time and may even work for some other companies, since I love the performing side of this business. I'm an ordained minister, so I may do more ceremonies as an officiant and I hope to continue to do speaking engagements and maybe a few workshops, but really, when I retire, I want to do only what I want to do."

Ah, diversification. That may be the secret to longevity in this business.

"Being a DJ is really a young man's game"—Hugo Drax,

In Prospect, Connecticut, Mobile DJ Keith Alan, who will be turning the big 6-0 this month, is as busy as ever with wedding receptions, game shows, and several kids-themed events. Even though he is reaching that milestone and has been a Mobile DJ since 1982, he is still only runner-up in the age game in his area.

"I am the second oldest DJ in my market that I am aware of," Keith says. "The majority of my competitors are in their 40's." Yet he continues to fill his calendar. "While there are a lot of younger disc jockeys in my market, I'm still very busy. One of the things that keeps me working is my attention to professionalism."

Unlike Randy, retirement plans for Keith have not been given much consideration yet. "To be honest, I haven't made any real retirement plans. I guess when the time comes, I will fall back on my ability to marry couples as a Connecticut Justice of the Peace and move towards the managing part of the business." He concludes, "As long as couples book me, corporate people see my age as experience and kids like to play games," he will continue on.

In their combined 58 years in the Mobile DJ business, neither Randy nor Keith has ever seen a DJ carry on to that golden age. "I've never met a Mobile DJ who actually retired. I've met many who quit being a DJ, but usually they just go back to their day job as their only source of income," says Randy. And Keith adds, "Since I'm blazing the trail for the younger guys, seeing a fellow DJ retire hasn't happened yet."

The way I see it, the point Hugo Drax was making is this: Prepare yourself. The end of your music spinning days is coming, and for most it will be sooner than that magical number listed on your Social Security statement. His summary may have been a hard dose of reality to swallow for some, but as the leader in the world's largest trade organization for DJs and karaoke jockeys in the world, he's fulfilling his obligation to give them the truth.

Wedding photographers, bridal shop owners, and wedding coordinators would all be wise to take note.

Chapter 20

Sometimes a Mind Changes

(January 2016) December 22, 2015—My daughter tied her shoes all by herself yesterday. We all celebrated this amazing accomplishment. You might be thinking she's a 5-year-old, since that's when children usually develop their shoe-tying skills, but she's not. She's 19. Why is she learning this skill now? How does this all fit into the DJ world? Read on . . . .

In early November, *Disc Jockey News* publisher John Young invited the staff writers and some other key members to Vadnais Heights, Minnesota, for our annual conclave. This one though would be a little different from previous events. Whereas previous conclaves resembled a sort of mini DJ convention with seminars, speakers, and product displays, this one would focus on more round table business discussions, some of which would be recorded for the *Disc Jockey News* Virtual DJ Expo. One of the sessions—recorded by Jeremy Brech, Bill Hermann, and Mitch Taylor—discussed the importance of balancing family and business.

"In our business it's really hard for our significant others, and especially our children [to] understand what we do and why we have to put so much time into it, and not just on the weekends but everything that goes on in the week as well," Jeremy said in his opening.

The words made me pause, probably more so than they would have a year ago. I had always prided myself on being an active parent in our children's lives. Throughout their years of growing up I had never missed a parent–teacher conference, I chaperoned field trips, volunteered backstage when they were involved in a school production, and even worked as editor for the school newsletter and served on the PTO Board while they were in middle school. That's a pretty impressive résumé, if I have to say so myself. But that's not to say I was always there. There were birthday parties that I missed, family anniversaries that my wife attended alone, and those milestone moments I missed like seeing my son or daughter all dressed up and leaving for his or her first Homecoming or Prom. If I had heard Jeremy's words one year earlier, I probably would have used them to justify missing those key moments. But things have changed in the past year.

Megan, our middle child and oldest daughter, was the overachiever of the family. Several times my wife and I joked that we needed to have her DNA tested because she was nothing like us when we were in school. In her middle school years she participated in mock trial, the dance team, the school musicals, color guard, show choir, and was on a "Battle of the Books" team that won the school district championship all three years she participated. In high school she continued with many of those activities; in addition, she served as student ambassador and helped tutor a foreign exchange student. In May, a panel of her educators voted her to be one of two students to deliver commencement addresses to her graduating class of over 400 and an additional crowd of nearly 2,000. In her speech she said, "Please remember: The least important things in life are the most important. The finest details create experiences, moments, and memories." Those were words that would ring in my ears just months later.

During her final two years of high school, Megan began to limp. We attributed it to the effects of constant bustle on her leg. Our family doctor sent us to an orthopedic doctor who treated it as tendonitis, then a jumper's knee, and sent her to a local physical therapist. Knee creams, cold packs, and exercises did nothing to make a difference. Then this past summer my sister, who is a nurse and a long-time physical therapist herself, was home for our son's wedding and noted how Megan was limping on her leg. "There is something more going on than just tendonitis," she commented. Before returning to Reno, she did her own assessment on our daughter's leg and asked us to take the results to our family doctor. He concurred with her notes and decided to send her to a neurologist for an MRI.

By this time, Megan was attending the University of Northern Iowa, where she had been selected to join their color guard squad. We decided to have the MRI done there for the sake of convenience. What they discovered was that there was nothing wrong with her leg at all. Instead, she was diagnosed with cavernoma, which is essentially a benign brain tumor, resting on the motor skills cortex of her brain, which was affecting her left leg.

Our only option was to have the cavernoma surgically removed, so we met with a team of doctors at the University of Iowa and set a surgery date for December 11 so our daughter could complete her first semester of college.

"Please remember: The least important things in life are the most important. The finest details create experiences, moments, and memories."—Megan Lenstra

On December 10 we all made our way to Iowa City. We were told that the surgery could take over six hours and might actually leave her left leg weaker, so we took a pair of crutches to the hospital to be prepared for that scenario. What we were not prepared for was that the surgery not only weakened her leg, but actually left her with no sense of touch or movement at all on her left side. She was in essence completely paralyzed on that side of her body. Slowly, though, the sensations began to come back. Four days after the surgery she could stretch out her left leg and move her thumb. The following day she was transferred to a rehab center in one of our hometown hospitals. By day six she could open and close her left hand and bend her left knee. And yesterday, 10 days after the surgery but still in the hospital, she tied her own shoe, and we celebrated the accomplishment!

The doctors cannot give us a definitive prognosis. How many of her motor skills she is able to retrieve and how long that will take is like predicting the winner of next year's Super Bowl. You may be able to make an educated guess but there is just no way of really knowing. They tell us that her chances of returning to school this year are very minimal, and that she will not be coming home for Christmas. That's okay. We'll just keep all the presents under the tree and keep the decorations up until she does—even if it takes until January.

Her spirits, though, continue to soar . . . in part, I believe, because of the overwhelming support she is getting. High school friends come by the carload. College friends drive an hour and a half to come see her. Staff members from a local community theater where she interned during the last two summers keep popping in and bringing her gifts. There seems to be a party going on in her room every night. The physical therapist has helped her to stand for a while, then with assistance to walk. Yesterday they asked her to walk 50 feet with their assistance. She achieved that— and then asked if she could try the steps. Sheer determination is what is going to bring her back 100%.

Now to answer that question: How does this fit into the world of Mobile DJs? The way I see it, it's sometimes too easy to lose sight of what is really important. I see many of us get so caught up in the competition of having more gigs, newer gear, and especially more money than others in our business that we forget who we really do it all for. For years Mobile DJ icon Randy Bartlett has encouraged us to be just 1% better for the benefit of our clients. Do we also apply those principles to our family? Songwriter Neil Diamond was once quoted as saying, "When you're on the merry-go-round you miss a lot of the scenery." Scenery we take for granted maybe, like watching our children tie their own shoe. Sometimes it might be best to let someone else on the ride for a moment.

The late great author Stephen R. Covey (*The 7 Habits of Highly Effective People*) once said, "The main thing is to keep the main thing the main thing."

What is that for you?

Epilogue

Thank you for reading.

The stories and lessons I've learned and shared in the previous pages are the ones that have been most memorable to me and/or have influenced me the most as I have traveled the Mobile DJ road for over 25 years, primarily as a wedding entertainer. For the past seven years, I've had the good fortune of sharing these stories and lessons with the readers of the *Disc Jockey News*. I hope those readers—and you, the reader of this book—have found them to be entertaining, as well as providing you with what is always referred to as a "nugget" that may be able to help you along the way in your own Mobile DJ career.

I compiled this book because I wanted to leave something behind in hopes of making a difference, like so many others in this field have done for me. I feel very blessed to have been able to exercise two of my passions in life—DJing and writing—and have been able to make my living from the former for the past several years,

The sections of the book and the chapters within those sections follow no particular order or significance—except for the last two. I wrote Chapter 19, "It's an Age-Old Question," in August of 2014. As I'm getting older, and nearing the end of my career, it's a topic that I now give a lot of thought to and visit from time to time.

I thought it would be fitting to include near the end of the book. In June 2018, I did a follow-up article to that and re-interviewed many of the principal players from the first article. I concluded each interview by asking for a bit of parting advice. Keith Schulz of Keith Alan Productions in Waterbury, Connecticut, left me speechless with his reply, for he said nothing of how to make more money, or plan for the future, or how to leave a legacy.

"Put your family first," he said. "Any type of money that you earn can be replaced, any type of equipment can be purchased again, but your family is the most precious thing that you'll ever have, and if you lose the time with them that's something you'll never get back."

Boom!

And that segues into Chapter 20, "Sometimes a Mind Changes," a personal story about my daughter Megan. That article probably got a bigger response than anything else I have written. Rather than leave you in limbo, I should let you know how things turned out: Megan returned home from her surgery on New Year's Eve 2015, and we celebrated the new year by opening Christmas gifts the following day. She was not able to return to school that year, but instead had to endure seven months of intensive physical therapy. She was determined though to make it back to school and rejoin her color guard team. The coach, bless her heart, said they would welcome her back and find a place somewhere so she could get on the field for a routine or two, maybe not really expecting her to ever be able to be a full participant again. She surprised us all by not only making it back, but she participated in every event from beginning to end for the next two years, She will always have some paralysis on her left side and there are things she will never be able to do again, like ride a bike, swim, or run, but that does not seem to deter her. Not only did she complete those two seasons with the color guard team, she participated in a couple of the school plays, became a student ambassador to the incoming freshmen, was hired to be a part of the school's orientation staff over the summer months, and still continuously makes the Dean's list. In her senior year she was named the University of Northern Iowa's Homecoming Queen.

For me, now that I see the sand in the hourglass of my DJ life getting emptier, my goals have changed. I no longer base my thinking on how many weddings I can book or if I can increase my bottom line by X% this year. Instead, my preference is to book enough events to continue making my living at what I still love to do while still finding ways to take off enough weekends to spend time with the family as well.

I encourage you to do the same.

Acknowledgements

I've always felt that my accomplishments were achieved with the help of many, (but my failures I own all on my own). It takes a lot of good people to be successful in any endeavor and I'd like to acknowledge many of them here that have been so critical to me.

First, to John Young, publisher of the *Disc Jockey News:* Thank you for the opportunity.

To Chris Feldman, who has been my proofreader/editor for years. I always say he makes me look smarter than I really am. Thanks, Chris.

To Dave Dunnam, my own personal tech support line, thanks for everything.

To all of those who have been part of the Alexxus Entertainment staff over the years: Bob, Steve, Brian, Ted, Rhett, Doug, Keith, Tim, Chris, and Marcus. Thank you for representing my dream so well.

Thanks as well to Greg Birkett and the staff at the Dubuque Advertiser for encouraging me to take this journey so many years ago and allowing me to basically begin it in my corner office while I was still an employee there.

To all the people who contributed their thoughts and opinions to these articles and are mentioned within them, thank you.

Many people in the industry have greatly influenced me over the years, none more so than Ron Ruth. He has become a great mentor, a good friend, and someone who I consider the shining star on the staff of *Disc Jockey News* writers.

To Lisa Blodgett, who has helped guide me through this process of self-publishing a book—thanks.

To my children, Alex, Megan, and Emily, who have been so understanding while their father has been away or holed up downstairs working, thanks for your patience.

And finally, to my wife Laurie, who has voluntarily become a weekend widow all of these years and allowed me to do what I truly love to do. None of this is possible without you. You know what they say, behind every successful man . . . I love you always.

ABOUT THE AUTHOR: Michael J. Lenstra is a self-described Wedding DJ and is celebrating 25 years as owner of Alexxus Entertainment in Dubuque, Iowa. For the past seven of those years he has also been a monthly columnist for the *Disc Jockey News* authoring the column *The Way I See It*.

[022319]